s the heart-crushing news that your
ıallenges, the waves of grief threaten
; exact journey that *How to Build a
Thriving Marriage as You Care for Children with Disabilities* is
such a welcome light in what is so often the darkest valley. Filled
with hope when you need it most—and many practical action
and relational steps you can take right now—this new book gives
couples the perfect roadmap for thriving in the midst of troubled
times."

Matt Jacobson, founder of FaithfulMan.com,
and **Lisa Jacobson**, founder of Club31Women.com

"For any couple whose relationship is crumbling under the grief
and stress of parenting children with disabilities, these pages offer
priceless hope and help. Todd and Kristin Evans speak with in-
sight and honesty about their experiences and how to rekindle
love, faith, and partnership in even the most hurting marriage.
It's not too late to make a new way forward, together, and this
book shows the way."

Rob and Joanna Teigen, founders of
Growing Home Together and bestselling authors

"At last! A marriage book written specifically for parents of children with disabilities and special needs. Todd and Kristin Evans
offer hope born of personal and professional experience and show
couples how to assess and strengthen different aspects of their marriage in simple and powerful ways. Had *How to Build a Thriving
Marriage as You Care for Children with Disabilities* been written
when my husband and I were raising our medically fragile child,
it would have been on our bookshelf. I hope it will soon have a
place on yours too."

Jolene Philo, national speaker and coauthor of *Sharing Love
Abundantly in Special Needs Families* (with Dr. Gary Chapman)

"*How to Build a Thriving Marriage as You Care for Children with
Disabilities* is one of the most thoughtful and practical books
on creating and maintaining a healthy marriage while caring for
someone with a disability. Todd and Kristin write from experience
and show deep wisdom and understanding of the challenges. It is

a must-read for parents, professionals, and anyone working with families where disability is present."

Rev. Tom Jones, executive director of the Faith Inclusion Network

"Kristin and Todd Evans have created an excellent resource for couples struggling to keep their marriage alive while also parenting a child with significant limitations. The Evanses don't sugarcoat their hardships, including major mental health and financial crises, but use them to address the primary conflict areas for disability-affected marriages. They provide couples with detailed guides for problem-solving, skill-building, and learning how to destress together. If your marriage is suffering due to your child's disabilities, this book can serve as your compass to a renewed relationship with your spouse and help you both find your way to a life filled with joy."

Catherine Boyle, mental health ministry director, Key Ministry

"If you are married and caring for a child with disabilities of any kind, this book is a must-read! Todd and Kristin have woven together years of research, wilderness survival training, life experience (the good, the bad, and the ugly), and Scripture to produce an incredibly encouraging and practical guide for marriage. As a special needs dad, a husband, and a ministry leader of families for nearly thirty years, this is one of the best books I've ever read on marriage for special needs parents."

Steve Chatman, vice president of Rising Above Ministries

"Todd and Kristin were the guest speakers at the Wonderfully Made Family Camp for special needs, and they poured into the parents to strengthen their relationships and marriages. They are transparent about their journey and how they drew closer to God and to each other. What a gift to see the blessings, find the joy, and build strategies to make their marriage stronger but then want to help others who are on similar paths. God has prepared them for this journey, and it will be amazing to watch how God continues to use Todd and Kristin, along with their book *How to Build a Thriving Marriage as You Care for Children with Disabilities*, to bless families around the world."

Beth Castile, Wonderfully Made Family Camp coordinator
and special needs ministry advocate

HOW TO
BUILD A
THRIVING
MARRIAGE
AS YOU CARE FOR
CHILDREN WITH
DISABILITIES

HOW TO

BUILD A
THRIVING
MARRIAGE

AS YOU CARE FOR

CHILDREN WITH
DISABILITIES

KRISTIN FAITH EVANS, MA, MS, LMSW
AND **TODD EVANS,** PHD, MA

BakerBooks
a division of Baker Publishing Group
Grand Rapids, Michigan

© 2024 by Kristin Faith Evans and William Todd Evans

Published by Baker Books
a division of Baker Publishing Group
Grand Rapids, Michigan
BakerBooks.com

Printed in the United States of America

Library of Congress Cataloging-in-Publication Data
Names: Evans, Kristin Faith, 1980– author. | Evans, Todd (William Todd), 1978– author.
Title: How to build a thriving marriage as you care for children with disabilities / Kristin Faith Evans, MA, MS, LMSW and Todd Evans, PhD, MA.
Description: Grand Rapids, Michigan : Baker Books, [2023] | Includes bibliographical references.
Identifiers: LCCN 2023036743 | ISBN 9781540903730 (paperback) | ISBN 9781540904188 (hardback) | ISBN 9781493445745 (ebook)
Subjects: LCSH: Parents of children with disabilities—Religious life. | Marriage—Religious aspects—Christianity. | Parenting—Religious aspects—Christianity.
Classification: LCC BV4596.P35 E934 2023 | DDC 248.8/45—dc23/eng/20231031
LC record available at https://lccn.loc.gov/2023036743

This publication is intended to provide helpful and informative material on the subjects addressed and is not a substitute for seeking professional counseling or mental health advice from a professional. Readers should consult their personal health professionals before adopting any of the suggestions in this book or drawing inferences from it. The author and publisher expressly disclaim responsibility for any adverse effects arising from the use or application of the information contained in this book.

The authors are represented by the literary agency of WordWise Media Services.

Cover design by Laura Powell.

Baker Publishing Group publications use paper produced from sustainable forestry practices and post-consumer waste whenever possible.

24 25 26 27 28 29 30   7 6 5 4 3 2 1

For our two beautiful children,
who have shown us what is most important in life.

Contents

Note to Readers

Dear Couple,

Marriage is hard. Add in children with disabilities, and a thriving marriage may seem impossible. Maybe you've lost the joy, closeness, or fun in your relationship. Your life is probably so consumed with just trying to survive all the demands of caring for your child(ren) that your marriage hasn't been given the attention it needs. You may be managing to get by day-to-day, or your marriage may be crumbling around you.

As disability parents, you are on a unique journey that is challenging and can easily break your marriage. It nearly broke ours. Yet by persevering through the pain and struggles, we've discovered that we've actually grown closer and reached a deeper level of marital satisfaction than we could have ever imagined possible. We want you to experience the same results, but with less of the stumbling and pain we endured in trying to figure it all out.

We're going to share with you a unique set of evidence-based skills for building your marriage while caring for your child(ren) with a chronic medical condition, autism, a mental health disorder, a physical impairment, or other special needs. Research and experience have shown that you need additional skills to improve your marriage. Yet studies have also shown that if you invest in your marriage, there's a good chance your relationship will become more fulfilling and resilient than the average couple's. So, we want to come alongside you as your guides to help you navigate this challenging terrain. You don't have to do it alone. We hope to inspire you with stories, encourage you with Scriptures, and challenge you with research-based tools to actively build your marriage so you can discover a life of deeper joy and meaning together.

We know you're likely exhausted, and trying to find the time to invest in your marriage might feel overwhelming. We also don't want you to have to research one more issue; we've scoured the professional info and will guide you in building the additional skills that are critical for couples raising children with chronic illnesses and disabilities. These tools have empowered our marriage and the marriages of other caregiving couples as well. We've intentionally created this resource to feel as simple and practical as possible.

This isn't the kind of book you can pick up and read cover to cover. In fact, we recommend you read one chapter at a time and work on building that set of skills together, as you can. Depending on your circumstances, you may need to slowly work on developing the skills. And that's okay. Think of it as a journey. This resource is more like a survival skills manual than a book. Go at your own pace.

You've already taken the first step toward building a thriving marriage by reading this letter. Watch your relationship grow stronger as you commit to digging in and learning the skills and then practicing them. At the end of each chapter, you will find an exercise to complete together. If you faithfully work on building the skills, we know your marriage will improve and you'll discover the amazing life God has in store for your future together.

We realize that disability parents have differing terms they prefer to use. We have chosen to primarily use the word disabilities, *because we have observed the community transitioning to this language.* Disability *is also the legal terminology that qualifies an individual for services, benefits, and accommodations. But we also want to be sensitive and as inclusive as possible, so we will use the terms "disability parents," "special needs parents," "medical parents," and "caregiving couples" interchangeably.*

We hope you will feel our support and encouragement as you work through this resource. As you continue further with us, we'll help you catch a new vision for how your marriage can be the catalyst for a better and more fulfilling life.

Blessings on your marriage journey,

Todd and Kristin

Reorienting Your Marriage

1

Survey Your Surroundings

Recognizing the Need
for Additional Marriage Skills

I will make a pathway through the wilderness. I will
create rivers in the dry wasteland.

Isaiah 43:19 NLT

We were jolted awake in the dead of night; our red eyes met one
another's panicked expressions. We were instructed to get out of
the van. In the dark, we could just make out the silhouettes of
tall trees surrounding us. Confusion and fear gripped us. Looking around, we discovered we had been dropped off in the middle
of the wilderness with just a pack of supplies, a compass, and a
topographical map. The first day of our graduate school internship had begun.

The first couple of days together in the wilderness were rough.
We wandered and argued, but we did finally learn how to work as

a team and began to move forward. By the end of the fourteen-day trip, we were thriving and hiking joyfully. But to begin bonding and making progress, we had to first gain some new wilderness skills. We had to learn how to use a compass, build a shelter, and purify our drinking water over a fire. And we had to relearn how to work as a couple in our new and challenging environment.

We felt a similar disorientation when we brought our medically fragile baby girl home from the neonatal intensive care unit (NICU). Everything suddenly became different and unknown. We were overwhelmed, and it seemed like our marriage switched from cruising to crisis mode. We had no guides. No trail markers. No instructions. The two of us were left to figure out how to survive together. We stumbled and argued in a "relationship wilderness" for years.

Now, twenty-two years into our marriage, we look back and marvel that our marriage survived our daughter's early years. How did we find a way to love and support one another and live with joy while in a seemingly impossible situation? We finally recognized how lost we had become and determined to move forward together. What we didn't realize was that we needed someone to teach us the additional relationship skills we required for our marriage to thrive.

You may feel like you've abruptly woken up in the wilderness and are still disoriented, as you've just been given the difficult news about your child. Or you may have been stumbling in the wilderness for months or years and may even be caring for more than one child with disabilities. You might feel ragged and worn out, with little hope that your marriage can survive much longer. Perhaps one of you feels alone in the wilderness, like your spouse has given up and abandoned you. Regardless of where you are in your relationship and how long you've been there, our goal is to help you reorient your marriage and move forward together. You can begin growing stronger and closer as a couple on your unexpected journey together.

The Need for Additional Marriage Skills

The first five years after our honeymoon were some of the most exciting times of our lives. We were in love, and nothing could stop us from pursuing our dreams and living the adventure of our life together. We talked, we went on dates, and we stayed home and binge-watched our favorite shows. We even packed up and moved to the foreign land known as the Chicago suburbs to attend graduate school together. Eager to see our marriage thrive, we read marriage books, joined a newly married couples Bible study, and even went to a marriage conference. And then we worked to put those principles into practice. Our marriage was going great, and it all seemed so easy.

Then things changed. Five years into our marriage, our lives turned from the bliss of young love to the day-to-day grind of caring for our son, who had a rare medical disorder and complex needs. A little over a year later, we realized we weren't doing well as a couple. We argued more than we laughed or smiled together, felt hurt more than loved, and even began to imagine what life would be like apart from one another. So we found a marriage counselor and went to therapy together. We read the marriage book he recommended and tried to apply its concepts as best we could in the midst of our chaotic lives. It helped a little and allowed us to reconnect some. But our relationship still felt more like a business partnership than an intimate marriage.

Two years later, we were ecstatic to learn we were pregnant again. But then a bombshell hit. The geneticists counseled us that our next baby could be born as the fourteenth-known case in the world with the same genetic metabolic disorder as our son. Yes—fourteenth. But the doctors would know how to test for the disorder immediately after birth and how to treat it. However, the pregnancy quickly turned into a nightmare roller coaster. We discovered that our unborn daughter didn't have our son's metabolic disorder but a completely unrelated and much more severe condition. In that moment, we switched into crisis mode—mentally, emotionally, physically, and spiritually—and our marriage entered a vast wilderness.

During this time, Kristin was in the hospital for two months, and we were daily reminded that our unborn daughter would likely not survive. We desperately tried to keep our three-year-old son's life as normal as possible despite the tumult. After a traumatic emergency delivery, we held our miracle daughter, Bethany Grace. But then we watched her suffer through two sets of surgeries, prayed as we witnessed her crash into respiratory arrest, and celebrated as she came back to life and improved.

We knew from our experience with our son that it was going to be very challenging to care for Bethany Grace at home. But nothing could have prepared us for how our lives would flip upside down. When she came home from the NICU at three months old, we shut down every other area of our relationship to simply make it through each day and keep our daughter alive. The stress began to tear us apart. We operated as separate individuals just trying to get everything done while caring for both of our children's extensive needs. We were paralyzed and in shock. We stopped talking about anything other than caring for our kids. We stopped caring for one another.

Years went by, and we just kept living in crisis mode. We'd failed to acknowledge or accept our difficult circumstances, and validating one another's painful emotions had gotten lost in the daily stress. As a result, we hadn't found a way to move forward together. We kept hoping things would get better if we only made it to the next day.

Our marriage was in critical condition. We hadn't gained the additional relationship skills we needed to stay close and keep our bond strong. We didn't even know we needed to work on special marriage concepts. We thought that returning to couples counseling and addressing traditional marriage principles, such as listening to one another and resolving conflict more lovingly, would solve our problems and fix our relationship. We learned the hard way that this is not the case for many marriages with children with disabilities. And the statistics we heard gave us little hope we would be able to save our marriage.

Be Encouraged by the Facts

But let's debunk the popular myth—there's not an 80 percent risk for divorce for parents of children with disabilities.[1] Our marriage wasn't doomed, and neither is yours. Researchers don't agree on an exact rate for separation, divorce, or marital dissatisfaction for couples parenting children with chronic illnesses or special needs. Several factors influence the risk of failure for these marriages, and results are variable. Numerous studies report a range from no increase in risk to up to two times the risk.[2] Yet other studies have found that a significant number of couples report their marriage has grown stronger and they enjoy increased intimacy as a result of caring for their child with disabilities.[3]

The research may be inconclusive, but professionals do agree on one fact: caregiving couples face increased, unique, and intense stressors that parents of typically developing children usually never experience.[4] There *is* greater strain on our marriages. Disability parents are also at significantly increased risk for developing mental health disorders and chronic health conditions, which can also lower marriage quality.[5] As a result, caregiving couples must use different coping skills and use them more often than parents of children without health complications or disabilities.[6]

You see, when couples care for a child with additional needs, their relationship also needs additional supports. This is due to the added and extraordinary stressors pressing on the marriage. The more strain put on your relationship, the more resources and attention your relationship requires if you want to grow a healthy, loving marriage. As a couple, it's critical you learn additional relationship skills so you can remain strong on your new and challenging journey together. You certainly can enjoy a close and fulfilling relationship even as you care for your child with special needs. In fact, we believe that through building these supplemental marriage skills together, your relationship can be even stronger and more intimate than it would have been if you did not have a child with disabilities.

Survey Your Marriage

The first step to getting out of crisis mode and moving forward in your relationship is assessing the current state of your marriage. You have to identify where you are starting from and what resources you already have to know where you need to go and how to get there. Once you've gotten your bearings and surveyed your present reality together, then you can begin to see and accept that you are in the wilderness and plan how to thrive in this new and challenging environment.

Focusing on your daily challenges can make it difficult to remember to use your resources. Look at your resources. You do have some basic supplies and gear. However, every couple's pack has slightly different contents. What resources do you have? Hopefully, you have a safe and stable place for your family to live, enough food on the table, and warm clothes. You may even have the support of some family and friends or respite care.

But most importantly, you've been given a compass. You still may be wandering around from day-to-day like we were, not knowing which direction to go. In caring for your child with disabilities, there's likely no clear path, trail markers, or even a defined destination. What's more, many serious detours can pop up in your way. To know which direction to go, you must first orient to north. We believe God is the ultimate True North. We've experienced the power of God's provision, guidance, and help in our marriage and family. Trust God to point you both in the right direction. And your map? The Bible. God's Word is a lamp for your feet and a light on your path (Ps. 119:105). Reading Scripture will help you understand God's heart and desire to heal your marriage, give you strength, and show you how to love each other daily.

No matter how lost you are, how dire your marriage crisis seems, how hopeless you feel, or how wide the ravine feels between the two of you, God has not deserted your marriage. In fact, he cares so deeply for your marriage, he's still holding it together. You may not feel like you have the strength left to love each other anymore, but God will help you. All the supplies you will need, he will provide. Ask for anything you need. Allow God to fill your hearts until they overflow. We hope you will come to know "how wide and long and high and deep is the love of Christ" (Eph. 3:18).

More than anything else, your compass and map will help you on this difficult journey together. If you're able to let God guide you toward True North, read Scripture, and commit to building some new skills, you will learn how to thrive in the wilderness together and begin to discover new strength and joy on your journey. The wilderness of disability parenting may be challenging, painful, and dangerous at times. Yet being out there is also beautiful and wonderful, and you can experience magnificent views that can only be seen in the wilderness.

Before you read further, complete the Disability Parenting Marriage Assessment Tool in the appendix. This assessment tool will guide you through an examination of the different areas of your relationship. Our intent is not to overwhelm or discourage you. Every marriage has strengths and vulnerabilities. As you assess each area of your marriage, try to identify your strengths and current skills as well as areas that may need extra attention. The following chapters will build on your responses in the assessment. So please take the time to complete it! Up ahead, we will go deeper into all the areas discussed in the survey and help you gain the skills you need to address the challenging places in your relationship.

Pray Together

God, we come to you exhausted and maybe even hopeless. We want to trust you to help us strengthen our marriage. Please fill us with your love so we can love one another. Help us to know where to start and teach us the skills we need to grow our marriage on our disability parenting journey. We know that you can do "immeasurably more than all we ask or imagine, according to [your] power that is at work within us" (Eph. 3:20). Thank you for your great love and grace. In Jesus's name, amen.

2

Embrace Your Unexpected Journey

Recommitting to Your Vows

Love never gives up, never loses faith, is always hopeful,
and endures through every circumstance.

1 Corinthians 13:7 NLT

Kristin: Three years of twenty-four-hour caregiving and financial strain had nearly ripped our marriage apart. We had no desire left to spend time together. We could barely even stand to be in the same room.

But a friend from church had persisted in her offer to stay with the kids so we could go out on a date night. We sat down in the car and shut the doors. Uncomfortable silence filled the space between us.

"Where would you like to go?" Todd turned to look at me.

"I don't know." I really didn't care to go anywhere.

He backed the car out of the driveway. We didn't speak a word as he drove with no destination in mind. We eventually ended up at the lakeshore.

Gazing out over the moonlit water, I confessed my heartbreaking conclusions. "I don't want to be married to you anymore. We're not going to be able to heal from this and move on." Tears streamed down my face.

Todd took my hand. "I haven't given up on us. I'm never going to leave you. I believe in you. I believe in us."

Emotions flooded me. After all that I'd said and done to hurt him, he had just renewed his wedding vows to me. A spark of hope and love that I hadn't felt in years began to grow that night.

Realizing Your Lost Dreams

Couples typically stand at the altar in the sight of God and their closest family and friends with dreamy visions of a wonderful future together. Newlyweds don't usually envision a future of traumatic loss, constant challenges, chronic illnesses, or extreme strains on their marriage. But when couples have a child with disabilities, medical complications, or mental health disorders, suddenly "for better, for worse, for richer, for poorer, in sickness and in health" takes on a whole new meaning, and these vows are tested in unimaginable ways. Life may look drastically different from how you had pictured your future together. Your disappointments are more extreme than most couples ever experience or can imagine.

When we were engaged, we knew what we wanted for our lives and our marriage.

Todd: I want twelve kids. I can't wait for family gatherings through the years with all the grandkids running around.

Kristin: We'll be free to work together in full-time camping and adventure challenge ministry and missions, maybe even overseas. As the directors of a camp, we'll watch our kids playing in the creek and in the woods.

Todd: We're going to have so much fun together. Every day after work we'll play tennis, watch movies, ride bikes, and hike. This will be incredible, living life with my best friend.

Kristin: I love dreaming about the new places we'll visit together and as a family. We're going to live life to the fullest.

Those were the dreams we cherished as we lay on a blanket in the park and planned our future together. With the challenges that have since come with disability parenting, we've had to say goodbye to many of them. For years, we felt disappointed, confused, and sad. Our unmet expectations caused frustration and conflict between us. But eventually we learned to embrace our circumstances, make drastic adjustments, and find new ways to enjoy life together.

Accepting Your Circumstances

Practicing acceptance will be the key to moving through loss and disappointment to find hope, meaning, and joy. Willingness to embrace your child's condition and the implications for your life and marriage means that you acknowledge your circumstances as they are, not as you imagined they would be or as they once were. Acceptance doesn't mean you will no longer grieve or be sad. Acceptance is not agreeing or disagreeing that this is how things should be. Rather, acceptance is simply agreeing that your circumstances are reality and letting go of the struggle against it.

Choosing an attitude of acceptance will help you adapt to your new reality. Remaining in nonacceptance will create distance and conflict between you.[1] Award-winning clinical psychologist and author Dr. Marsha M. Linehan explains, "Refusing to accept reality can keep you stuck in unhappiness, bitterness, anger, sadness, shame, or other painful emotions. . . . Acceptance may lead to sadness, but deep calmness usually follows."[2] The deeper a couple's level of acceptance, the easier it will become to talk about loss. Growing in acceptance and processing your emotions will lower your levels of stress and depression and improve your marital satisfaction.[3]

The aim is to balance coping with your loss while fully living your present life.[4] Acceptance will be a continual journey in tandem with chronic sorrow. You may still be grieving your loss while embracing what you currently have. In one moment you feel both sadness and joy, and in another moment disappointment and gratitude. Allowing yourself to acknowledge all of these emotions and share them freely with one another will help you heal. The more you can accept your situation, the better adjusted and more resilient you will be as a couple.[5] Honoring your sorrow while embracing your present circumstances will give you a fuller perspective on life. It will allow you to envision a hopeful and enjoyable future together.

Our God promises you, "'For I know the plans I have for you,' says the LORD. 'They are plans for good and not for disaster, to give you a future and a hope'" (Jer. 29:11 NLT).

Readjusting Your Expectations

Not only are disability parents grieving the loss of their hopes for their child and family, but they've also realized that some of their expectations for their marriage relationship may never become reality. The future you dreamed of together likely didn't include the challenging circumstances surrounding caring for your child with a chronic illness or disability. Simple goals and plans are much more complicated now and may not be practical or even possible.

To be resilient as a couple, function well, and grow closer, you'll have to adapt.[6] Adapting will include readjusting your expectations for how your marriage relationship and life together will look. As disability parents, we need to reorient our marriage expectations to our new circumstances. You will have to restructure your way of thinking as a couple and adjust to the new norm. This will be a continual process.[7] The more you're willing to be flexible and adjust, the more resilient your relationship will be.

Look at your original expectations for your marriage and consider the new parameters around your child's care needs. Whittle down your old expectations and goals to those you might be able to achieve given your new reality. Is there a way to modify or adapt your hopes and dreams? Maybe you both dreamed of prominent careers. Now one of you might pursue a career that fits with your family's situation while the other sacrifices a dream to manage the needs at home. Perhaps you had planned on having more children, but now you fear your next child could have the same condition or you might not be able to care for an additional child. You may need to adjust your original expectations. That kind of choice hurts, but it may be necessary.

As you continue to grieve the loss of many of your dreams and goals, replace them with new ones you can work toward together that will fit into your new journey. By grieving your lost dreams for your marriage—your disappointments, your now impossible plans, and your crushed expectations—you will be able to move on to reimagining your new future together. It may become possible to reintegrate some of your dreams in the future. But for now, it's time to adapt and let them go.

Mending Your Wounds

Kristin: Following our son's medical crises, I knew his development wasn't typical. I spent hours researching and working to get him into good specialists for evaluations. But Todd resisted my attempts to discuss the issue or consider that I could be right. As we were painting our son's new bedroom, the emotional pressure cooker exploded into one of the worst arguments we've ever had. I will never forget the words he fired at me: "You just want something to be wrong with him."

His accusation pierced my mother's heart at the core of my already bleeding wound. Not only was I hurting for my child but my husband had just invalidated and insulted me. He was doing nothing to help me get our son the interventions he desperately needed.

Todd: My response that day stemmed from a combination of frustration with the situation, the time and attention Kristin was spending on our son, and my own denial about the seriousness of our child's needs. It took months, but I slowly came to accept the truth about our son's condition and realized how desperately Kristin was trying to help him and how much she needed my support and involvement. It was hard to admit that I was wrong and apologize, but for the good of our child and our marriage, I knew I had to ask for forgiveness and begin supporting Kristin more.

Kristin: Those words and Todd's lack of support for months deeply wounded our marriage, but I've since healed and forgiven him. At the time, I don't think he fully grasped how much he hurt me, but he sincerely expressed regret, and I accepted his apology. I understand now that we were both coping the best we could during an extremely stressful and emotionally painful time.

Apologize to One Another

As you prepare to continue your journey together of disability parenting, assess any lingering hurts still not cared for. Otherwise, as you travel, your resentment will fester and grow deeper. Begin the journey as healthily as possible. With all the stress and grief you've endured, it would be surprising if each of you hasn't been hurt or doesn't have something for which you need to apologize. Spouses do things they normally wouldn't to escape painful emotions and unbearable pressure.

Here are several common hurts caregiving parent marriages experience, including more severe issues:

Saying harmful or unsupportive statements.

Detaching from your spouse emotionally.

Invalidating your spouse's grief.

Not helping with caregiving and parenting.

Working too much in order to avoid being home.

Intentionally withholding sexual intimacy.

Ignoring your spouse's mental health concerns.

Suggesting separation or divorce.

Escaping through pornography.

Having an extramarital emotional or sexual affair.

You likely don't even realize all the ways you've hurt each other. Honestly tell your spouse the ways you've been hurt. They simply may not be aware. Also confess any secrets you may have kept from each other. Guilty or shameful thoughts tell you to hide. But hiding will continue to create distance between the two of you. This is the time for you to lay everything out on the table. On this challenging journey, you can't afford to carry any extra emotional weight. When apologizing:

Acknowledge the hurt and validate your spouse's feelings.

Sincerely ask for forgiveness.

Ask your spouse what they need from you.

Ask what you can do differently next time.

Avoid becoming defensive.

Plan how to avoid this same hurt in the future.

Forgive One Another

In order to heal, you must also be willing to forgive each other. God calls us to "clothe [ourselves] with compassion, kindness, humility, gentleness, and patience" and forgive one another as the Lord forgives us (Col. 3:12–13). Forgiving does not mean you agree that what they did or said was right. Being willing to forgive means accepting their apology, letting go of blame and bitterness, and no longer holding their wrongdoings against them. This will not happen instantly. Depending on how deep the wound is, it may take time to rebuild trust and intimacy.

The wonderful news is that we don't have to go through this process on our own. God is love, and our forgiveness comes from him. With his help, grace, and power, we can forgive and rebuild

31

Some of these hurts may be severe and require additional help from a counselor to work through your problems. If you feel like the two of you cannot resolve your issues on your own, seriously consider going to a marriage therapist. Even if you believe you can reconcile and move on without help, your marriage will likely still benefit from counseling.

trust as we confess our sins to God and to our spouse. The Lord, our wonderful counselor, "heals the brokenhearted and bandages their wounds" (Ps. 147:3 NLT). Remember, wounds don't heal overnight. Forgiveness and healing will be a process. Simply remain faithful, patient, and supportive of your spouse's process. Let go of the hurt and hold on to one another.

Recommitting to Your Wedding Vows

We wrote our own wedding vows. But at no time while writing them did we ever think to imagine they should include the words, "Through chronic hospitalizations and surgeries, through trying to not go bankrupt, through spending our days at therapies and specialist appointments, or through constantly trying to just keep our child alive."

Now that you have a fuller picture of your joyful, painful, hard, yet beautiful path ahead, it's time to wholeheartedly recommit to your relationship. You committed to your wedding vows unconditionally—and you have stuck to them. If you had the opportunity to include an addendum to your wedding vows describing your current, specific, unique circumstances, what might you write? "Through extreme financial strain, through challenging behavioral interventions, through endless therapies and appointments, through less time together, through grief and chronic sorrow, through unbearable stress . . ." What would you add?

Although you're experiencing more challenging circumstances than you ever thought to imagine, you can discover a deeper level of commitment and closeness through your struggles than you may have thought possible. Your future as a couple may not be what you imagined. But perhaps what's most important is not where this path of special needs parenting is taking you but that the two of you are on this journey together. Recommit and clasp hands.

Reflect and Recommit

1. Grieve your lost dreams for your marriage.

What are some dreams for your relationship that you feel you've lost?

Wife:

_____

_____

Husband:

_____

_____

Share your lost dreams with one another and grieve together.

2. Move toward acceptance of your circumstances.

What aspects of your life are you having difficulty accepting? What dream feels the hardest to give up?

Wife:

_____

_____

Husband:

_____

_____

3. Readjust your expectations.

Together, choose one unrealized expectation that you shared for your married life. Brainstorm ways you can modify or simplify your plan to make it feasible. (For example, if you enjoy going on long bike rides together but cannot be away for a full day, you could consider biking together while pulling your child in a bike carrier.)

Unrealized expectation:

_____

Ways you can adjust your goal or plan:

_____

_____

4. Tend to any emotional wounds.

What are some ways that you may have hurt your spouse for which you need to apologize and ask for forgiveness?

Wife:

_____

_____

Husband:

_____

_____

What are some ways your spouse has hurt you for which you desire an apology? Are you willing to forgive them and heal?

Wife:

_____

_____

Husband:

_____

_____

Do you feel any guilt or shame that you have hidden and are afraid to share with your spouse? If so, about what?

Wife:

_____

_____

Husband:

_____

_____

What steps do the two of you need to take to recover and prevent this hurt from happening again?

_____

_____

_____

_____

5. Apologize to one another.

Begin the healing process by apologizing and forgiving one another. Truly offering and accepting may take time. Do not feel pressured to complete this process during one sitting but come back to it as needed.

6. Recommit to your marriage vows.

Add an addendum to your vows to speak to your most specific challenging circumstances:

"Through _____,
through _____,
through _____."

Now recite those promises to one another: "I promise to love you and stay by your side through . . ."

Pray Together

God, we are sad and disappointed. Many of the dreams we had for our life together are no longer possible. Help us to see our marriage and our future together from your perspective. Give us hope and help us to embrace our new life. With your help, we recommit to staying together, by one another's side, on this journey of parenting our child. Thank you for your strength and love. In Jesus's name, amen.

3

Repack Your Packs

Setting Priorities and Reorganizing Your Day-to-Day Responsibilities

Carry one another's heavy loads.

Galatians 6:2 NIrV

We've led a lot of groups on backpacking trips over the years, and we've discovered that not everyone shows up prepared to start hiking. So, the first thing we do when a group shows up at the trailhead is have them dump everything out of their bags. Inevitably, someone has brought impractical supplies like a six-pack of soda, a cast iron skillet, makeup, a camping chair, or other nonessentials. These items are all great for everyday life or a normal car camping trip. But for a strenuous trip in the wilderness, these items can make the journey more difficult. Not only that, but there are also special tools and supplies they forgot to bring or didn't know about, like a water filter, fire starters, and medical supplies. Our job as guides is to help participants remove items that will weigh them down and add necessary items they might have forgotten. In the same way, our goal is to help you reorganize your life based on your priorities so you can manage your day-to-day activities and have time to strengthen your marriage.

Inspect Your Packs

Imagine you are sitting in the woods by a river. You both have a pack in front of you. Peeking inside, you see your packs are already full of supplies. Each item represents a responsibility that the average married couple with children typically manages—employment, childcare, kids' activities, housework, paying bills, and home, car, and yard maintenance.

But now you need to stuff in all the additional jobs you juggle as disability parents. Turning around, you discover these extra supplies on the ground beside you. Now, add items to your packs for doctor, counseling, and therapy appointments. Pick up more supplies for school meetings and phone calls to insurance, pharmacies, supply companies, and providers. Pack items for medical caregiving, assisting with activities of daily living, and managing challenging behaviors. Add more for the time needed to give siblings extra support. Don't forget extra provisions if cooking meals takes longer due to allergies, sensory aversions, or feeding disorders. If you have extra laundry due to toileting accidents or feeding tube leaks, pack that too. At this point you might feel like investing in your marriage is just something else you need to squeeze in, even though it's your most valuable resource. But how can you place your marriage first and fit everything else in?

And how can you muster the strength to carry these heavy packs? The answer is you can't—at least not the way they are currently packed. And you're not alone. Parents of children with special needs typically have more responsibilities and spend more time caregiving than parents of children without disabilities. These demands tend to crowd out the time, energy, and patience needed to have a healthy marriage. Caring for a child with chronic illness or disabilities creates an imbalance in routines and family functioning and destabilizes the marriage relationship.[1] If you attempt to manage life as you did pre-diagnosis, it will only frustrate you, create more stress, and potentially do damage to your marriage and family.

For disability parents to be resilient and positively adapt, they have to adjust to the new norm and additional caregiving demands and strengthen their management and organizational skills.[2] It's time to look at all the tasks you're trying to stuff in your packs and make sure they line up with your priorities. This process can be challenging. So, we have broken down the exercise into four steps and explain each one. For now, simply read through the steps. At the end of the chapter, you will have the opportunity to work through the repacking process together.

Step 1: Identify Your Priorities

You already know you can't cram everything in your packs, which means some things are going to have to go. Determining what needs to stay is much easier when you have established priorities in your life, and you use them to help direct your decisions. Work together, but each of you should make your own list of the greatest concerns you have for your family. Your lists may include your children's health and development, your marriage, your faith and church attendance, spending quality time as a family, and so on. As you compare your lists, you will see some commonalities as well as some differing ideas. The concerns that resonate with both of you will form the core of your priority list. If you haven't already, make sure your list includes items that involve self-care, mental health, specific times to build your marriage, and social support activities. These areas are vital for your individual and marital health. Combine all your priorities into one list to use as a guide as you assess and reorganize your life.

Step 2: Empty Your Packs

Now, dump out your packs and assess everything the two of you have been trying to carry. Grab a stack of sticky notes and a couple of pens. Each spouse should write down all the jobs and tasks for which they're individually currently responsible. Write only one job or task per sticky note. This is a brainstorming session, and there are no wrong answers. The most important goal is to write down as many aspects of daily life as you can. Also add notes for any tasks that are necessary but have been neglected. Make it a game to see who can come up with the most notes. Perhaps the "losing" partner changes the next diaper or washes the dishes.

Now that you have everything out on the table, you can see how big your pile really is. It may feel overwhelming, but it's also awe-inspiring to see how much you actually have been doing. Give each other a pat on the back and say, "You're doing a great job." Then get back to working on taking control of your life together.

Step 3: Lighten Your Load

Note: For this step, we prefer the tangible exercise of holding and moving the notes, but if space is limited or you prefer to create an electronic spreadsheet, you can adapt the exercise to how you naturally work best.

Pick a wall in your house where you can temporarily post all these notes undisturbed. Then divide the space into three areas. The rightmost area will be for all the sticky notes that are aligned with your priorities. The leftmost area will be for activities that don't line up with your priority list. The middle area is for any you are unsure about. Have your priority list handy so you can easily reference it. Begin working together to place all your sticky notes into one of the three areas. As you place notes in the middle area, discuss them and help each other decide where they need to go. If you can't quickly reach a decision, just leave it in the middle and move on. You don't need to agree on how to do it all at this point. You just want to identify anything that does not line up with your agreed-upon priorities, because those things will weigh you down.

Now, remove all the notes on the left side of the wall and put them in a box or folder labeled "Not right now." It may be painful to put those notes away, but you can have hope that there may come a time to add a few of those activities back into your life. You may not be able to plan that romantic getaway to Europe right now, but hopefully it'll happen someday. For now, you need to put these things aside so you can focus on the activities the two of you decided are the most important at this stage of your life.

Continue lightening the load by looking at each responsibility and task on the wall and seeing if it's something only the two of you can do. A task like communicating with doctors would likely

It's critical to remain optimistic throughout this process, knowing that you *will* be successful at figuring this out together.[3] But we want you to know that this process will likely be challenging. Being vulnerable in this way and honestly talking about these difficult and emotionally charged issues might become intense. You may experience conflict and hurt feelings. Resentment regarding how tasks have been delegated up to this point may surface. Commit to creating an emotionally safe atmosphere free of judgment and criticism and make an extra effort to listen to one another and support each other throughout this process.

If you notice your discussion becoming unproductive or stuck on past hurts, gently refocus your attention to completing the present activity. If problems and conflicts seem to be more than you can handle right now, feel free to jump to chapter 5 for conflict resolution skills and then come back. Be willing to apologize, forgive, and have grace with one another. Above all, approach this process with love, patience, kindness, gentleness, and self-control. Use 1 Corinthians 13:4–5 and Galatians 5:22–23 as your guide.

fall on this list. But other jobs like mowing the yard or cleaning the house might be something you can ask other family members or friends to help with, or you can hire out if you have the money. Maybe your ten-year-old can start helping more with the dishes, or a good friend can take your child to an occupational therapy appointment. Consider having your groceries delivered. Even one small timesaver can make a big difference in your stress levels.

Also ask your church or churches in the area if they have any ministries that could help you or if they know of anyone who might be able to support you. Different churches have ministries that help families with yardwork, car repair, ramp building, house handiwork, transportation, or meals. For example, when Bethany Grace was first home from the NICU, a retired lady from our church came to sit next to her crib so Kristin could work on other tasks or even just take a shower. (In chapter 6, step 3, we suggest some local resources that may be available to you.)

It can be difficult to accept help, but if someone asks how they can support you, don't be shy in accepting their offer. Give them specific ways that are at your comfort level. If your house looks anything like ours, letting people see the mess can take courage. But remember, accepting help is going to improve the well-being of your marriage, mental health, and family. When it comes down to spending your time repairing the home or having more time with your spouse and child, asking for help makes sense. If you can find ways to get help, delegate, or hire out chores, this will allow you time to focus on the other priorities in your pile that need *your* attention.

One final way of lightening your load is to consider making major changes in your life that will make it easier to manage everyday stress. For us, Kristin stepped down from her job to be at home, allowing for more time to handle all the children's care responsibilities. Eventually we even moved cities to get closer to the specialized medical care our children needed rather than driving four hours each way several times a month. Todd made multiple career changes to allow him more flexibility and availability to help with the family. Big decisions like these should not be approached lightly. We spent over two years discussing and praying about our move before God opened the doors and provided an opportunity for us. Pray fervently about these decisions, communicate openly with one another, seek the counsel of people you trust, make a joint decision, and step out in faith when the time is right. Those changes in our life made a huge difference in our family and marriage. Similar changes might also help you.

Step 4: Repack Your Packs

There will still be a lot of notes left on the wall, but remember you are on this journey together. You each have your own pack to share the load. So, with those notes remaining on the right side of the wall, write your name on each one that you would like to champion. Try to be flexible, open-minded, and willing to compromise. Consider your strengths. Choose roles that you're passionate about or tasks where you have strong skills.

Kristin: Without question, Todd's much better at managing the finances and paying the bills than I am. He's amazing at budgeting and saving money. He even organizes all the bills in a database so we make sure to pay them on time. We could work on the finances together, or I could probably do okay on my own, but he can do it so well in a fraction of the time. I choose to trust him.

Todd: Kristin's much better at understanding medical terms and knowing the complex history of each child. So, she keeps up with all the specialists and takes the kids to most of the appointments. If I take them because of scheduling issues, I'm on speaker phone with Kristin while talking to the doctor to make sure all the important issues are communicated and that the plan fits with our children's care needs.

You might decide that you would like to take turns sharing a certain role. In this case, create a duplicate sticky note so you each take one for the task. The more flexible you can be in sharing some roles, the more your relationship satisfaction can increase.[4] It's important to mention that you both need a sticky note for caregiving and parenting. We realize you will likely not be able to share this role fifty-fifty. One or both of you may be employed full-time, and one of you will likely need to be the primary caregiver. But both of you must spend some time in the development of your child and helping with caregiving.[5] We explore this important issue in more detail in chapter 11.

Inevitably, there will be tasks left that no one really wants to do, but go ahead and split them up between you. You might want to keep in mind that when spouses share the housework, they both report higher satisfaction with their sex life.[6] And remember: make sure to include self-care activities and time as a couple in your packs.

Stop at the point when you're not sure you can take on more or you agree that you just don't know how to do what's left. Have each spouse gather up all the notes with their name and reposition them on a section of the wall off to the side. Make a separate area for each spouse. This will help you better see and understand how much each of you will be doing. Look at each other's responsibilities and discuss how the load feels. Consider swapping some sticky notes or redistributing some tasks to make the weight feel reasonable for both of you. Talk openly during this process. It's crucial that your new plan for the daily routine is sustainable, based on your goals and values, and meets the needs of your marriage and family.[7]

You might also be left with another group of notes that you just don't know how to deal with. You might not have the time, money, or resources to manage them. Those kinds of issues are going to take more work and creative solutions, and we are going to help you with those in chapter 6. You are also going to have to trust God to help you take care of some of those issues. He is faithful to provide a way when one doesn't seem possible. Depend on him to help lighten your load. He calls to us, "Come to me, all you who are weary and burdened, and I will give you rest" (Matt. 11:28).

Now you have divided up the list of responsibilities and day-to-day activities for your family, and you are carrying them in your packs. By organizing and assigning roles, you will be more efficient and able to accomplish more. You will also be able to grow and enjoy your marriage. By intentionally choosing how you will spend your time and resources based on your priorities, you can move forward confidently on your journey. You are ready to set out together.

Reflect and Repack

Ready to get started? As needed, you can refer back to the full explanation for each step. Go through this process together in a way that works best for the two of you. We suggest using sticky notes, but if you prefer to create an electronic spreadsheet or to process in a different way, go with what works best for you.

Step 1: Identify Your Priorities

1. Each of you make a separate list of the greatest concerns you have for your family and other activities important to you.
2. Now, share your lists with each other and note commonalities.
3. On a new piece of paper, make one combined list of the aspects of life that you both think are important. This is your priority list.

You've made some great progress in starting your priority list. Feel free to continue to add to it as you think of additional shared priorities. You will need some supplies for the next section and that may take a little time, so take a quick break. If you need to come back to this later, set a time within the next forty-eight hours when you can meet to work on this step.

Step 2: Empty Your Packs

1. Grab a couple stacks of sticky notes and pens.
2. Write down every job or task for which you have been responsible (one per sticky note). Also add notes for necessary jobs that have been left undone. Think of as many tasks as possible, even small ones.
3. Lay out all of the notes in front of you to see how much the two of you have been doing. Say to one another, "You have been working very hard. You're doing a great job."

Step 3: Lighten Your Load

1. Pick a wall and designate the right side for all the notes that align with your priorities, the middle section for notes you are unsure about, and the left side for notes that do not align with your priorities.
2. Place each note in one of the sections.
3. Take off the notes on the far left side and place them in a box or folder labeled "Not right now."
4. Brainstorm ways to ask for help, use services or resources, hire out, or delegate tasks to other people.
5. Begin discussing any major changes you may need to consider making.

Step 4: Repack Your Packs Together

1. Begin writing your name on sticky notes for jobs or tasks for which you want to be responsible. If it is a task the two of you would like to share, create a note for each of

you. Remember to consider your strengths and be open-minded, flexible, and willing to compromise.

2. Gather all the notes with your name on them and put them in separate piles.

3. Discuss how the load feels for each of you and if you need to adjust and swap notes.

Pray Together

God, sometimes it feels like the weight of the responsibilities in our lives and all we have to do is more than we can bear. But we know you promise us rest when we come to you with our heavy burdens. Help us set aside thoughts and unnecessary distractions that weigh us down. We confess we sometimes put our own desires ahead of your plans. Show us what is most important in life and encourage us to focus our time and energy on those things. Teach us to put our priorities in line with yours. In Jesus's name, amen.

Building Additional Marriage Skills

Setting Your Bearings

As you finished section 1, we hope you've found a new perspective on your life together and your future path ahead. You've recommitted to one another even though your new journey isn't what you expected and may have been emotionally exhausting. Now, you must be intentional about building the skills that will help your marriage and family thrive.

Section 2 is all about building the specific skills you need to adapt and grow your marriage through the challenges you're facing. As you look at the figurative wilderness of your lives or perhaps the literal wilderness of your marriage, it's easy to get lost or overwhelmed. When you're out in this terrain, you can't just hope to get to where you want to go. You have to be intentional about heading in a specific direction, or else you will find yourselves wandering and exhausted. In hiking, this is called "setting a bearing." It's a powerful process to help keep you on the right track. We want to use the same idea to help you stay on the right path to a joyful marriage.

Setting a bearing is all about breaking up the journey into smaller, more manageable pieces. You pick a place that's not too far away and line your compass up in that direction. Next, you take a reading of your compass and then use that reading to help point you in the proper direction. Remember, God is True North and will help guide you. Once you reach your spot, you pick a new one, take another compass reading, and then continue the process—over and over again. All the while, you're getting closer and closer to your goal destination as you successfully work through each step.

We want you to approach the skills in section 2 in the same way. Each chapter teaches a skill that will be a small step on your overall journey toward a stronger marriage. Don't get overwhelmed by trying to fix your marriage all at once. Instead, work on each chapter one at a time first by reading through it, separately or together. Then set a time to meet and go through the application section at the end of the chapter. The exercises will guide you in how to apply each skill directly to your marriage by going through the three steps of "setting a bearing."

 ## Step 1: Identify Where You Are

Every couple will find themselves in a different starting place for each of the skills and goals in the following chapters. The first step is to determine where your marriage currently is in reference to each specific skill. For instance, in chapter 5 we focus on the skills of improving communication and deepening emotional intimacy. For one couple, the starting point might be trusting their spouse with a painful thought. Another couple might be healing from an extramarital affair, and just beginning to talk openly may be a major step toward that goal. We've found that most couples don't even know how bad or good aspects of their marriage are until they specifically talk about them. Once you're able to identify where you are in your marriage for each specific skill, you can move on to setting realistic goals.

Step 2: Set Your Goal

For each of the marriage skills in section 2, we want to guide you in setting and achieving a specific short-term goal that will be critical for functioning as a couple and thriving in your marriage. Your marriage goal for each skill should be a stretch for you, but attainable. For instance, perhaps a couple wants to have more respite time together (see chapter 8). They decide getting away for a night is too much right now, but if they work at it, they think they can get out of the house for two hours to have coffee. So, they set two hours as their goal. After successfully getting away for coffee, they can later decide if they want to set a new goal of a night away together.

Step 3: Plan Your Path

Once you understand where you are starting from for each skill and have a defined goal to work toward, you can set a path to get there. This step is all about making practical plans and steps to move forward in developing the skill. It takes flexibility, creativity, and perseverance, but the rewards are worth it. Remember to use Scripture as your map. Continually referring to it will help you see the big picture.

Don't just stop at making a plan. Get going! Start working on it right away. As you take steps in working toward your goals for each skill, you will become more and more energized by the progress you're making. You will start to see areas of your relationship beginning to flourish, and it will transform your outlook on life and your marriage.

4

Cope as a Couple

Developing Healthy
Stress Management Skills

Two are better than one, because they have a good return
for their labor: If either of them falls down, one can help
the other up.

Ecclesiastes 4:9–10

It's an established fact backed by mounds of research: couples parenting children with chronic illnesses or disabilities experience *significantly* higher levels of everyday stress than couples parenting children without special needs.[1] What's more, one of the greatest predictors of marital satisfaction for caregiving parents is our stress levels.[2] One study found that couples of children with autism spectrum disorder (ASD) who reported lower levels of stress were 8.6 times more likely to experience relationship satisfaction than caregivers with higher levels of stress.[3]

Also, due to their added stress, parents caring for children with chronic illnesses or disabilities are at significantly greater risk for developing physical and mental health disorders, especially mothers.[4] Increased stress can also lead to marriage conflict, divorce, and family dysfunction.[5] We feel stressed and overwhelmed and have difficulty coping when our parenting roles and responsibilities are more than our personal resources can handle, whether that be our emotional coping skills, social support, or financial means.[6]

So, to increase your marital satisfaction and preserve your mental, physical, and emotional health, you must use specific coping skills and stress management strategies to get your stress levels down and then prevent them from rising back up. You need advanced ways to support one another and cope emotionally. Couples who have children with special needs must use more coping strategies more frequently than couples who have typically developing children, and these strategies are often different from mainstream approaches.[7]

When a couple uses good stress coping skills and engages in self-soothing activities, their marriage improves and they enjoy a closer and more loving relationship.[8] When a caregiving couple doesn't use healthy coping strategies, their marriage relationship can suffer.[9] What's more, if there are differences in how you are coping or one of you is having difficulty regulating your emotions, it will strain your marriage. But when a couple uses similar healthy emotional coping styles and adapts to stress together, they enjoy higher relationship and sexual fulfillment.[10]

There are two generally accepted approaches to managing stress: either eliminate or reduce the cause of the stress or learn more effective ways of coping with the stress. You likely cannot change your situation or many of your stressors right now, but by learning and applying new emotion and stress regulation skills, you can help your marriage thrive as well as better balance your emotions and lower your body's stress responses. When the tense moments begin to boil (and they will), you'll have more effective ways to cope together in the moment. Emotion-focused coping is when we use strategies to regulate our emotions and lower the impact that the stressful situation is causing.[11] The opposite of regulating our emotions is becoming more upset or dysregulated and engaging in some type of unhealthy escape behavior, whether mentally, emotionally, or physically.[12]

The research shows there are specific coping strategies that make caregiving marriages more resilient. These are also the skills we've discovered and developed to help strengthen our own marriage. Let's work on building five of these empowering coping skills to help strengthen your marriage.

1. Find Strength in Faith

"Those who hope in the LORD will renew their strength" (Isa. 40:31). Imagine that the two of you are each hanging by a rope from a mountain ledge. Your ropes are fraying and your arms are tiring. It's difficult to stay close and help one another. You're not sure how much longer you can hold on. But then a third rope drops down. You take this rope and weave it between the two of yours. You're now both hanging from a stronger cord of three ropes. God's help is that third rope. When you feel like you're at the end of your strength in your marriage, God is still holding you together. "Though one may be overpowered, two can defend themselves. A cord of three strands is not quickly broken" (Eccles. 4:12).

Leaning on God's power and endless love saved our marriage. We discovered how depending on faith amid incredible stress and grief can bring renewed hope and joy. Our experience of finding new strength in our marriage through our shared faith is not unique. Studies have shown that sharing a healthy relationship with God and strong faith practices such as praying, reading Scripture, and attending church can help you cope more effectively, adjust better, lower your stress levels, improve your mood and mental health, and increase your marriage resilience.[13] Caregiving couples who rely on God and share faith practices also enjoy greater intimacy.[14] The opposite is also true; avoiding God or having a strained relationship with God has a strong link with poorer marital quality and mental health.[15]

One or both of you may be struggling with faith questions, anger with God, or spiritual confusion. Through leaning on your faith in God, you can work through these struggles to find meaning and grow spiritually. Faith increases hope. Strong hope and an optimistic outlook about the future of your marriage and your child's condition can significantly lower your levels of psychological distress and burnout, help with coping, and improve your marriage.[16] Regularly nourish your faith together, and you will keep your connection to God and your relationship strong.

Here are a few ways to depend on God together.

Say Short Prayers

Saying short prayers together can remind you to look to God for help in your marriage, give you hope and strength, and draw you closer. Here are some sample prayers:

God, how are we ever going to thrive as a couple? Please help us work through our problems together.

God, please help our marriage. We feel so far apart. Bring us closer together.

God, I have no energy left to love my spouse. Help me love him/her with your endless love.

If you don't have the words or the strength, try simply sitting in a moment of silent prayer together.

Post Scripture Verses

Pick out some verses from the Bible and write them down as a reminder and a source of strength. You can stick them on your bathroom mirror, over your bed, on the fridge, or anywhere they will catch your eye regularly. Here are three of our favorites from Psalms:

> May your unfailing love be with us, LORD,
>   even as we put our hope in you. (33:22)

> But I will sing of your strength,
>   in the morning I will sing of your love;
> for you are my fortress,
>   my refuge in times of trouble.
> You are my strength, I sing praise to you;
>   you, God, are my fortress,
>   my God on whom I can rely. (59:16–17)

> My flesh and my heart may fail,
>   but God is the strength of my heart
>   and my portion forever. (73:26)

Consider Other Ways

Although some of these activities may not be feasible for you, we encourage you to find one or two to try together.

Meet with a pastoral counselor together or on video chat.

Find a church with a disability ministry and go to a worship service together, watch a service online together, or listen to a podcast together.

Join an in-person or online Bible study with other couples caring for children with disabilities.

Listen to worship music together.

Make a prayer poster to hang on the wall.

Relying on your faith together will be critical in coping with your grief and stress and growing stronger as a couple. Daily dependence on God and one another will be a lifelong journey. But it's a path you're on together, and God is always with you, holding the two of you up.

2. Live Mindfully

"The Spirit of God has made me; the breath of the Almighty gives me life" (Job 33:4). Regardless of your current life circumstances, look around at where you are and take one moment at a time. Take one step together, then another. Looking ahead at the trail for the coming weeks or years can become ineffective. Worrying about the future fuels anxiety and raises stress levels. Similarly, when you keep turning around to relive the past, guilt and depression can follow you. Yes, the two of you have to plan ahead and honor the past. But once you've taken time to reflect and your plans are in place, notice your current surroundings and feel yourselves in your present day.

This is called "being mindful"—living in your present moment. A simple definition of *mindfulness* is paying attention in the present moment "as openheartedly as possible," without judging or reacting.[17] The opposite of being mindful is mindlessness—being absorbed in the past, ruminating over thoughts or stresses, or focusing on fantasies or anxieties about the future. It's not fully listening or paying attention to what you're doing or doing more than one task at a time.[18]

You can practice being mindful by:

Consciously observing what's going on inside you and around you.

Fully engaging in the present moment and doing one thing at a time.

Remaining nonjudgmental about what's happening, what's being said, and what you're thinking and feeling.

Choosing an accepting attitude.

Having compassion for yourself and others.[19]

Right now, you may feel like you're climbing a grueling, rocky trail rather than gazing at a scenic overlook. Feeling overwhelmed can make us detach from the present and fantasize about having a different life or future. At a given moment, we may be driving while also on speakerphone with the doctor, our child is screaming in the back seat, and a feeding pump or pulse oximeter is beeping. Our minds and emotions can only take so much. When we become stressed, our minds become less focused on the present moment, and we start to live on autopilot. This is just about one of the worst things we can do as disability parents, especially for our marriage. When we're not being mindful, we are not fully present with our spouse—not fully listening, not paying attention to their emotions or needs, and not fully enjoying being in the moment with them.

Focusing your thoughts on the present moment is one of the most effective ways to cope with your distress. Practicing mindfulness can help you:

Regulate your emotions.

Reduce chronic stress, anxiety, depression, and PTSD symptoms.

Improve your long-term physical and mental health and quality of life.

Increase self-compassion.

Adapt more effectively.

Accept your circumstances.[20]

Being fully present changes the processes, development, and connections in your brain, counteracting the adverse effects of stress.[21]

So, as you go about your day, if your mind wanders to your to-do list or an upcoming stressful appointment, gently bring your focus back to what you're doing in the present moment. When you take a shower or bath, fully stay there in your mind, feeling the hot water and steam, smelling the soap and shampoo, and listening to the sound of the flowing water.

The principles of Western psychology mindfulness can easily be adapted to Christian faith beliefs.[22] Christian mindfulness has been found to be even more effective in reducing stress and depression.[23] By intentionally becoming aware of God's presence, we can have an increased capacity to commune with God and sense the Spirit's leading.[24] Here are some simple ways to practice spiritual mindfulness:

Become aware of God's presence—inside you and all around you.

Just be with God, Jesus, and the Holy Spirit, not doing or saying anything.

Focus on breathing—inhaling God's breath of life and exhaling your worries and pain.

Surrender control to God—your thoughts, emotions, cares, and circumstances.

Meditate on a verse of Scripture.

Whisper a short prayer asking for God's help.

Receive God's mercy, grace, love, acceptance, and compassion for yourself and others.

Worship with psalms, hymns, or simple statements of praise.

Journal your prayers, thoughts, and emotions.

Mindfully walk outside in nature, aware of God's presence.

As you go about your daily tasks, remain aware of God's presence in each moment throughout all you do. In the seventeenth century, Brother Lawrence devoted his life to practicing the presence of God throughout his day, saying, "I turn over my little omelet in the frying pan for the love of God."[25] As you care for your child, wash dishes, or do laundry, practice knowing the presence of God.

As you begin to fully experience the present moment, you will be able to engage with each other in deeper and more meaningful ways. You will also be effectively coping together. Practicing mindfulness as a couple can also:

Enhance the romantic quality of your relationship.

Increase compassion, forgiveness, and understanding toward one another.

Help you adjust and function as a couple.

Deepen empathy, love, and your emotional connection.

Help you respond to stress, problems, and conflict together more effectively.

Improve your communication and attunement to one another.[26]

Living mindfully takes practice and intentionality. Gently remind one another to be fully present throughout the day as you talk and spend time together, care for your child, or complete menial tasks. As you further develop your skill of fully living in the present together, you will be amazed at how your time together will become richer and your connection deeper.

3. Destress Together

"He lets me rest in green meadows; he leads me beside peaceful streams. He renews my strength" (Ps. 23:2–3 NLT). Finding ways to destress and relax together is essential. When you relax together, you are coping together, which will strengthen your relationship. If you give each other gifts, consider massage gift cards. Massages can greatly help reduce stress and relax you. Here are some other ideas for how to soothe one another's muscles, minds, and emotions:

Enjoy a eucalyptus spray shower or scented bubble bath together.

Give your spouse a foot or shoulder massage.

Engage in sexual intimacy.

Go for a walk or jog together.

Lie on a heating pad or under a heated blanket together.

Drink hot tea while snuggling in a blanket together.

A very effective stress reduction tool for disability parents is practicing Mindfulness Based Stress Reduction (MBSR) exercises. MBSR combines meditation, deep breathing, focusing on the body, muscle stretching, and relaxation.[27] Below are brief introductions to several guided exercises that you can do together. These can be as short as one minute and as long as forty-five minutes, and all can easily be found online.

Cleansing Breaths

Slowly inhale through your nose for four seconds.

Hold for four seconds.

Slowly exhale through your mouth as if gently blowing through a straw.

Do this two more times.

Relaxation Hug

Take slow, deep, cleansing breaths together.

Hug silently for one minute.

Notice your partner's breathing.

Body Scan for Tension or Pain

Lie on your bed or the floor and listen to a guided body scan exercise together. The voice will lead you through noticing each part of your body from head to toe and observing how you feel.

Progressive Muscle Relaxation

Similar to a body scan, listen to this exercise as it guides you through tensing and relaxing each muscle group as you move down through your body.

The lemon squeeze exercise is a shortened version of progressive muscle relaxation:

Grab a lemon or a stress ball or pretend that you have a lemon in your right hand.

Squeeze the lemon as hard as you can for twenty seconds.

See who can squeeze the hardest.

Suddenly drop the lemon.

Switch hands and repeat.

You can use this exercise with any muscle group.

Eye Gaze

Sit in front of one another.

Take each other's hands.

Stare into each other's eyes for one minute.

Just be in the moment.

Mindful Treat

Find your favorite treat.

Go somewhere private—maybe even your closet.

Spend two minutes slowly eating your treat and enjoying every bite together as well as each other's company.

Practice a short exercise at least once a day to cultivate mindfulness throughout your day. Then, when stressors bombard you, you will be better able to reorient your minds to the present moment and be fully present with each other. Practicing MBSR exercises together can be very powerful. In tense moments, stop and encourage each other to practice one of the exercises.

Sensory Walk

Go for a walk together in silence.

Use all your senses to become aware of your surroundings.

On the way back, talk about what you noticed.

Guided Imagery Recordings

Find a comfortable position next to one another.

Listen to the voice as it leads you to imagine yourselves in a peaceful location.

Allow your minds and bodies to relax.

Alternatively, instead of listening to a voice recording, you can sit and listen to nature sounds such as ocean waves or a mountain stream.

4. Support One Another's Self-Care

"Therefore encourage one another and build each other up, just as in fact you are doing" (1 Thess. 5:11). In addition to being at higher risk for experiencing marital problems, caregiving couples have a much higher chance for developing long-term physical and mental health conditions. You have up to twice the risk compared to parents caring for children without health or developmental special needs.[28] We are on this journey to empower you to care for your marriage, and your individual well-being directly impacts the health of your marriage. The healthier you both are physically and mentally, the stronger your marriage will be.[29] By supporting one another in caring for your individual mental, emotional, spiritual, social, and physical health, you will both be better able to manage stress and have improved mental health.[30] Telling your spouse that you see the level of stress they're under and helping them reduce their stress levels will increase your relationship resilience considerably. Supporting one another in self-care can also help you appreciate each other more and strengthen your bond.

Bethany Grace was three years old when we first learned the term self-care. We learned just how critical it was for both of us to prioritize taking care of our own health, and we knew we had to make a way to invest in one another's health. Neither of us really liked running, but we decided to try something new. We both signed up for triathlons and running races for the first time. Why would we do that? Having the motivation to train for these races provided numerous benefits: a way to support and encourage one another, a shared goal, major stress reduction and a healthy way to cope, a sense of accomplishment, and improved physical health, mood, and mental health.

Helping each other care for our personal health has greatly contributed to the increased health of our marriage too. While we enjoy running together, we also help one another take time to exercise and enjoy other activities alone. We call this self-care alone time a "self-cation." We encourage one another to take this self-cation and sacrifice our own time to give each other this gift. As the recipient, we find it can be very hard to accept this break. But allow your spouse to gift you this time with no expectation of anything in return. Even just short respites can help lower your stress levels, improve your mood, and reduce symptoms of anxiety and depression. These breaks will also benefit your relationships with your spouse and child when you return more rested.[31]

You may feel like you can't find time for self-care. This is where the two of you can use problem-solving skills. When Todd was preparing for a Half Ironman, training for the race required a lot of time. Then he realized he could combine commuting to work and training. Some mornings he would run the eleven miles to work, and other days he would bike there and back. With traffic, biking there actually took about the same amount of time as driving.

At first, it may be difficult to take a physical and mental self-cation, whether it's a brief or extended break. You might feel guilty for being gone and not helping at home. But as each of you takes time to care for yourself more frequently, you will begin to see how much it helps other aspects of your marriage and family. You will begin to find joy in giving this gift to each other, and you both will benefit from the other's self-care.

Here are a few ways you can support each other's self-care:

Encourage your spouse to go for a walk or jog. Exercise can help prevent and improve symptoms of depression and anxiety.[32]

Make them a fruit smoothie.

Arrange a day or a couple of hours to give them a break.

Suggest they go out with a friend.

Give them a mini getaway (such as an uninterrupted bubble bath or time to work on a hobby).

Support them in going to the doctor and/or counseling.

Encourage their spiritual growth and faith practice.

Let them get a little extra sleep.

If possible, plan for them an extended self-cation of a night away or a short trip with friends.

Allowing your spouse these breaks will greatly benefit your relationship in the long run. By encouraging one another to care for your well-being, you are learning healthy ways of coping with stress as well as supporting the health of your marriage. Reducing your overall stress levels and coping as a couple will make you more resilient, closer, and happier.

5. Laugh Together

"Being cheerful keeps you healthy. It is slow death to be gloomy all the time" (Prov. 17:22 GNT). A few years ago, we went into Bethany Grace's room to wake her up from her nap. Boy, did we find a surprise! As we opened the door, a pungent wave overwhelmed our noses. Horror music played in our heads as we stared at the plastic panels enclosing her medical bed. She had fingerpainted every vinyl window, and not with watercolors. She had also given herself a special makeover.

We turned to look at one another, a mutual understanding of emotional pain in our eyes. We both wanted to sink down to the floor and cry. But instead, we did something different. We began to laugh so hard our stomachs hurt and tears rolled down our cheeks. Why did we laugh? We honestly can't remember who said what first, but it was something like, "Wow, she's quite the artist! Looks like she had fun." Or, "Her bed needed a good disinfecting anyway. You wanna bet how many wipes it's going to take?"

We set to work together to clean up both Bethany Grace and her bed. We could have argued about who'd forgotten to put her special leotard on her. We could have become bitter about not having a typically developing daughter. It would have been easy to let the situation frustrate and sadden us. But instead, we allowed lightheartedness to win. We were able to see beyond our negative emotions because we had begun to learn how to be fully present in our difficult situations rather than mentally going somewhere else.

By allowing ourselves to even just briefly and silently acknowledge our painful thoughts and emotions, we were able to feel positive emotions. The experience drew us closer rather than driving us apart. Since that day, we've begun to find humor in other parts of our relationship more easily, especially when things don't go as planned. What started out as intentionally cultivating humor has helped us have a naturally more lighthearted outlook on life.

Developing the technique of humor to manage your life stressors is a vital skill for your marriage. We realize that, depending on your child's health or developmental status, our suggestion might sound impossible or just downright wrong. Yet maintaining a humorous outlook can improve your coping and stress management, physical health, mental health, adjustment, flexibility, marriage, and family functioning.[33] Laughing will improve your mood, soothe your mind and body, reduce tension, and even trigger chemical reactions that will make you feel good and lower your levels of stress hormones.[34] Most importantly, these shared moments will bring you together both at the time and in the future when you share that memory.

Think about a recent intense situation with your spouse. How did you react as a couple? What was the outcome? Imagine what it would have felt like to connect with one another by taking a lighthearted perspective and creating an inside joke between the two of you. How do you think this approach might have changed your emotions?

We're not suggesting you make jokes at the expense of your child. Rather, we're proposing you find irony and reflect on the extreme nature of your circumstances, how the situation could be worse, or even something positive. Finding ways to insert humor into these challenging moments isn't going to be easy. But it's necessary. At first it may take intentional effort. Cultivating a humorous outlook is a skill that can take practice, but at some point, it will become more natural. Here are example phrases that could break the tension and help you laugh together:

"Just when we thought we'd seen it all!"
"We couldn't make that up if we tried!"

"At least _____."

"Can you imagine if he/she had _____?"

"Well, that didn't go like we imagined."

Thinking about common situations you face, what are some other comments you could make to lighten the mood? As you're able, also look for humor outside of your circumstances, such as in a movie, a meme, or with other people. Try to let yourselves see humor in the world outside of your everyday routine. The goal is to release the pressure valve and smile at one another. Laughing more will help you cope as a couple, help you feel better together, help you strengthen your bond, and give you more joy in life.

As you depend on God in deeper ways, live mindfully, destress together, support one another's self-care, and laugh more together, you will become more effective at managing stress in healthy ways and strengthening your relationship.

Build the Skills

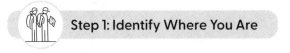 **Step 1: Identify Where You Are**

Assess your current stress levels and coping skills.

1. Rate your current stress levels.

Wife:

Not stressed at all	1	2	3	4	5	6	7	8	9	10	Very stressed

Husband:

Not stressed at all	1	2	3	4	5	6	7	8	9	10	Very stressed

2. How can you tell you're feeling stressed or emotionally dys-regulated?

Wife:

_____

_____

Husband:

_____

_____

3. How can you tell your spouse is stressed or emotionally dys-regulated?

Wife:

_____

_____

Husband:

_____

_____

4. What are two activities that help you personally cope with your stress and strong emotions?

Wife:

_____

_____

Husband:

_____

_____

Find strength in faith.

1. In what ways do you personally lean on God for strength?

Wife:

_____

_____

Husband:

_____

_____

2. What are some ways you rely on God as a couple for strength and help?

_____

_____

Live mindfully.

1. How often does your mind wander to the past, getting you stuck in guilt, regret, or traumatic events?

Wife:

_____

_____

Husband:

_____

_____

2. How often do you find yourself becoming anxious by worrying about the future?

Wife:

_____

_____

Husband:

_____

_____

3. What helps you stay engaged in your present moment?

Wife:

_____

_____

Husband:

_____

_____

Destress together.

1. How often do you destress together?

Never	Rarely	Sometimes	A lot

2. What are some ways you've found that help you destress and cope as a couple?

_____

_____

_____

Support one another's self-care.

1. How do you currently support your spouse's self-care?

Wife:

_____

_____

Husband:

_____

_____

2. In what ways does your spouse support or not support your self-care?

Wife:

_____

_____

Husband:

_____

_____

Laugh together.

1. How often do you laugh together?

Never	Rarely	Sometimes	A lot

2. What makes you laugh together?

Wife:

_____

_____

Husband:

_____

_____

3. What are some ways you've laughed together in the past?

_____

_____

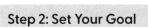 **Step 2: Set Your Goal**

As a couple, pick **only one** of the following types of coping skills. Focus on just that one at first. Trying to do more can overwhelm you and make it tempting to give up. When you are successful at learning one skill, then try a second one in the following weeks, and so on. If a skill doesn't seem helpful, try another one.

Find strength in faith.
Live mindfully.
Destress together.
Support one another's self-care.
Laugh together.

1. Which coping skill will you try together in the next two weeks?

_____

2. How will you practice that skill in your life and/or marriage?

Wife:

_____

_____

Husband:

_____

_____

Step 3: Plan Your Path

Plan a specific time that you will practice the **one exercise** you have chosen in the coming two weeks. This way you will already be familiar with the skill during more stressful moments.

Describe your specific time and plan for using the skill:

Day or time: _____

Plan: _____

Now, take the coping skill you have chosen together and put it into practice in the next two weeks. After you feel like you have begun to develop that skill, try adding another one.

Pray Together

God, sometimes we feel like we have no strength or energy left, and we can't keep going like this. When we feel stressed and overwhelmed, remind us to simply inhale your breath of life and exhale all our anxieties to you. Give us your grace to help us depend on you and find strength in you. Please fill us with your deep love for one another and show us how to relax together and support one another. Thank you for how you are already healing our marriage. We're relying on you. In Jesus's name, amen.

5

Check In with One Another

Deepening Communication and Emotional Connection

> You are my private garden, my treasure, my bride, a
> secluded spring, a hidden fountain.
>
> Song of Songs 4:12 NLT

Imagine that a couple of hours into a long hike together, you
notice a blister forming on your foot. Your spouse doesn't notice
your wincing, so you decide not to tell them. You begin to have
difficulty keeping up, but you just want to push on. Maybe you
fear your spouse will think you're weak or overreacting. Perhaps
you don't see the point of telling them, because they probably
can't do anything to help your blister anyway.

But if you don't tell your partner what's going on, you're not
giving them a chance to empathize with or help you, and the problem may worsen. No, they're not experiencing the same problem

or pain, and your blister may slow you both down. But the most important goal is being by one another's side at whatever pace. Therefore, you decide to tell them what's happening and how it feels. They don't understand how badly it hurts or know how to make it better. But they stop, tend to your wound, and comfort you. They support you through the next part of your journey together. As a result, you feel loved.

Had you not spoken up, the blister would have worsened to the point that it would have been difficult to finish the hike. You had to be willing to share your problem and pain with your spouse. Then your spouse had to be receptive, sympathetic, and supportive.

One piece that's missing from this scenario is that a regular check-in from your spouse asking, "How are you doing?" would have invited you to share your need. Also, if they had been paying attention to your facial expressions, they would have noticed something was wrong. If the roles were reversed, the needs would be the same.

Just as you would check in with your hiking partner, it's important to connect with each other at least daily. You need to see how the other is doing emotionally, what problems they're facing, and how you can support one another. You each also need to be willing to speak up and tell the other what you need and how you feel. We can become isolated from our spouse when we fail to communicate, and wounds that could have been prevented or cared for immediately begin to fester. However, sharing can lead to deeper connection and feeling loved.

As disability parents, there's so much you need to communicate about regularly. How do you triage which issues you need to talk about? When do you have time left to check in on your relationship? How can you move your conversations beyond just basic communication to deeper levels of sharing? Let's look at how to reenergize your relationship so you can communicate effectively and deepen your emotional intimacy.

Build Up Positive Emotions

Intentionally engaging in pleasant conversation and connecting emotionally will keep your feelings for one another positive. But due to the demands of your caregiving stress, you likely experience more unpleasant interactions than the average couple. These negative interactions accumulate over time and drain your relationship. Caregiving couples have to intentionally engage in a lot of enjoyable interactions to balance the harmful effects of negative ones.[1]

In his early years of researching, marriage expert and bestselling author John M. Gottman found that happily married couples typically engage in five positive interactions for every one negative interaction, especially during times of conflict.[2] Yet caregiving couples typically have less time and energy to spend with one another and share fewer enjoyable moments. One study found that, on average, couples with children on the autism spectrum experience only three positive interactions for every one negative interaction.[3] Negative interactions include criticizing, making angry comments, being sarcastic, and arguing. Positive interactions might include enjoying a fun activity, having a meaningful conversation, joking, flirting, showing affection, and giving/receiving compliments. When a couple has considerably more positive than negative thoughts about their spouse and their marriage, they can better withstand problems that come along.[4]

It's critical for special needs parents to look for opportunities to cultivate as many pleasant interactions with one another as possible. Stay in touch and regularly enjoy even short moments together. Some days are going to be more stressful than others and can quickly spark negative feelings. But if you're staying connected, you will be able to handle the heavier load together. You can boost your relationship mood by exchanging quick text messages just to say, "I love you," talking at lunchtime to check in, hugging, holding hands, stealing five minutes away to talk, sharing a joke and laughing, jumping in to help cook dinner, complimenting each other, or just sitting close to one another while completing different tasks. These little nonsexual touches, smiles, and moments will keep you connected.

We encourage you to find creative ways to insert these types of loving exchanges and romantic gestures throughout your day to let each other know how much you care. What little acts build positive emotions between you? If you don't know what actions mean the most to each other, ask. When you nurture positive feelings about your relationship, you have the mental and emotional energy to communicate more effectively and deepen your emotional intimacy. You have also created a base of trust and connection. You can be more perceptive, responsive, and supportive of one another.

Determine the Type of Conversation

There are several types of conversations that are important for couples to have: sharing thoughts and feelings, receiving mutual support, and engaging in problem-solving. As disability parents, you have two major additional conversational needs: coordinating all the additional daily tasks and discussing your child's support and service needs. All parents need to manage who's taking Johnny to school, Susie to soccer practice, and Harry to the dentist. For disability parents, these conversations are usually much longer, more complicated, and more intense. These types of conversations can easily eat up our time, pushing out the marriage relationship.

It's important to look at which types of discussions you spend most of your time engaging in. We are about to explore eight different types of conversations that are necessary for the health of your marriage and family. Numbers one through five can easily monopolize your time as special needs parents. These conversations are necessary and often urgent, but if you spend all your time on these issues, it will be challenging to reach a more intimate level of sharing. It will take intentionality and building stronger communication skills, but if you work as a team to become more efficient at the first five types of conversation, you will be able to prioritize spending more time strengthening your marriage through deeper conversations.

1. Coordinating Schedules

Conversations about coordinating daily appointments and tasks need to be as direct and efficient as possible to allow time for deeper discussions. Learn to be direct and ask specifically for what you need. You don't have the time or energy to hope that your spouse is reading your mind. When you agree to directly share your thoughts and listen to one another, you can avoid miscommunication, feel heard, and work to meet one another's needs as well as your children's.

One way to cut down on the time these discussions take is to share an electronic calendar you can both see and update. Make sure to communicate about any changes to the schedule. Another method is to keep a calendar on the kitchen wall. Take the time at the beginning of each month to list out all appointments, meetings, and so forth, and discuss who's taking whom where. Also, if possible, schedule short breaks and assign meal prep nights for both of you. This practice will save you time throughout the month in the mornings and the night before an event, which will also help lower your stress levels.

2. Chitchatting

Daily chitchat is also a place you can add in some extra positive interactions. Intentionally take advantage of any time you can connect as a couple. Maximize your opportunities to uplift and enjoy short moments together. Catch up over the phone while driving, or talk while cleaning up the kitchen, folding laundry, or caring for your child. Ask about something that interests your spouse and throw in some flirting or joking. These interactions will usually be short and lighthearted. Initiating these regular interactions throughout the day will consistently build a higher level of positive feelings between the two of you. It's unlikely that you'll often have large amounts of time together. So, making the most of these little moments throughout the day will be what helps keep you connected.

3. Planning Together

Going anywhere as a family can be complicated and require planning for how to accommodate your child's needs. Whether it's scheduling to go out to eat for dinner, to a friend's house, or on a vacation, you may need to talk through several issues. Then, when you are out in public, the two of you will need to stay in communication about monitoring your child's behavior or medical status. You may need to make decisions in the moment based on how your child is doing. Having these conversations in public can be difficult and cause tension between the two of you. Before going somewhere, talk through the potential issues and decide together ahead of time how you will respond. For example, your child might experience sensory overload. Decide ahead of time if one of you will take your child to a quiet place to calm down. Agreeing on an action plan beforehand will help prevent frustration, conflict, and resentment.

4. Discussing Your Child's Needs

You most likely will not agree on every aspect of your child's needs. This type of conversation can easily become divisive and take away from the time you need to spend building your marriage. It's best not to have these conversations on the spur of the moment or at stressful times of the day such as in the morning or dinner rush. Set aside a time when your child is out of hearing range (as well as you are able) to calmly discuss the issues. Before diving into one of these discussions, review the first part of chapter 11 about parenting as a team, and if needed, also review the conflict resolution section later in this chapter.

Begin by listing the things about your child that you are united on. For example, you both dearly love your child and just want what's best for them. Then give each spouse time to tell the other one way that they are a good parent. Now, calmly share what you think and feel about the issue in question. Openly discussing these issues about your child and making decisions as a couple will strengthen your bond.[5] You're under a great deal of parenting stress and possibly grief. Join as a team to give your child what they need and grow closer as a couple in the process. The more you invest in your marriage, the less divided you will be on these difficult issues.

5. Problem-Solving

You may need to discuss and resolve situational problems frequently and quickly adjust some days. For instance, when a nurse or caregiver calls in sick or your child needs to stay home from school, you will need to shuffle your schedules. Your problems can be from something as simple as needing to be in three places at once on a given day to not having enough money to pay the bills. Work together to find a solution as efficiently as possible. When you're facing issues that are causing stress, refer to chapter 6 for guidance through the problem-solving process.

As you become more skilled at these first five types of conversations, you will be able to spend more time engaging in the next three types, which are more intimate and relationship-building.

6. Checking In

Regularly checking in with one another will improve the health of your marriage and your mental health. It's necessary for disability parents to set a specific time to check in with each other that you can commit to every day. You need about ten minutes with no interruptions or distractions.[6] Guard this valuable time to ensure you regularly connect. Maybe you can plan to talk on your lunch break or after the kids go to bed. Whenever it is, you need to make sure you honor this check-in every day. This time should be more intentional than a chitchat. An easy but focused way to share about your day is to tell about one good moment and one bad one. As you listen to one another, communicate that you're listening, you care, and you're there to be supportive.

7. Sharing Thoughts and Feelings

This type of conversation is where you can intentionally build emotional intimacy, which is when you get in a positive cycle of both feeling safe to fully share your thoughts, emotions, wants, and needs, and you reciprocate acceptance, empathy, and understanding. As you both share and validate one another, you will draw closer and build deeper trust. You will also feel safer sharing in the future.[7]

This sharing can happen sporadically. For example, your spouse comes home from a hard day at work or your child's doctor's appointment and begins venting about an upsetting event. This is an excellent opportunity to listen, support your spouse, and build trust and connection. Put chores aside for a minute and give your child a preferred activity. Make eye contact with your spouse as they share about their day. It's crucial you take advantage of these moments to strengthen your relationship.

You will also need to intentionally make opportunities for these conversations to happen. It will take time to build deeper levels of trust and emotional security. Sharing thoughts and emotions and feeling supported by your spouse will nurture intimacy.[8] It's critical for spouses to accept and understand each other. When your spouse is vulnerable and shares on a deeper level, it's important to reciprocate and share something back.[9] When we feel confident that our spouse will accept us at our worst, we become vulnerable and share our deepest and darkest thoughts and feelings. This deepens intimacy even more.

When we nurture a more intimate connection, we also become more willing to share our most personal hopes and dreams. When your spouse shares intellectual ideas, career goals, or personal aspirations, you can support them in finding ways to work toward their hopes and to continue developing as an individual. Dreaming about your future together will be important as you grow stronger as a couple.

It's also important to share and discuss how you both feel about physical intimacy. You may not usually enjoy these types of conversations, or the discussion may usually not go very well. However, by practicing the skills in this chapter, you will build the foundation of trust and emotional intimacy needed to feel safe having these talks. Make sure to read chapter 9, where we dive into how to talk through and grow sexual intimacy.

Here are some good tips to help you learn how to more effectively share your thoughts and feelings.

Identify Your Communication Needs

When we first got married, we had a difficult time communicating without arguing and couldn't understand why. We turned to marriage books to try to improve our communication. It was when we listened to the audiobook of *Love Talk* by Drs. Les and Leslie Parrott that we learned a relationship-altering concept.[10] The authors assert that in general, men and women have different communication approaches and needs. Men tend to analyze and want to problem solve, and women tend to empathize and are looking to share emotions.[11] These findings are similar to the results of numerous studies of parents and couples caring for children with disabilities. Researchers have found that when coping with disability parenting stress, in general women tend to use a more emotion-focused coping style and desire time with their husbands to express feelings. In comparison, men tend to utilize action-oriented, rational, and instrumental behaviors to problem solve.[12]

We had an *aha* moment when we realized that when Todd brought up a troubling situation, he was almost always looking for help analyzing the problem to find a solution. He was seeking advice. When Kristin shared an upsetting situation, however, she was almost always first looking for empathy and emotional validation. When we didn't receive what we needed, we became hurt, defensive, and angry. We felt like the other person wasn't listening, didn't understand, or didn't care.

We had to learn to stop and ask, "Is this a 'solutions' conversation or a 'feelings' conversation?" Sometimes we were already into the conversation and saw our spouse's face and realized we needed to stop and ask. Other times we had to gently remind one another by saying, "I just want a feelings/solutions conversation right now." By implementing this simple practice, we have learned to be sensitive to one another's communication needs and connect on a deeper level.

Over the years, we've come to believe this practice is an especially important tool for caregiving couples. With the chronic, even daily, painful emotions and complex problems these couples face, developing this skill is crucial. We've concluded that for most situations, both partners, the marriage, and the family as a whole can benefit from having *both* a "solutions" and a "feelings" conversation about a given issue.

We have begun to express and need both approaches—Todd more feelings and Kristin more solutions. While each person prefers one approach over the other, we've discovered that our natural tendencies and skills balance one another out and make us a more effective team.

When your spouse comes to you wanting to talk, it might be easy to automatically respond with a question or statement in your preferred type of conversation—either solutions or feelings. An easy but powerful replacement response can be, "That sounds really hard. How can I help you?" This statement uses both a feelings and a solutions approach, which leaves it open for your spouse to respond as they need to. Try to remember to stop and first ask each other, "Is this a 'solutions' conversation or a 'feelings' conversation?" You will get to experience how powerful this practice really can be.

The feelings and solutions concept may not fully resonate with you, or the roles may be reversed. What's most important is that together, you identify your communication needs and the ways you typically respond to one another. Think through these questions:

When you're stressed and want to talk to your spouse, what do you need from them, and how do they typically respond to you?

What does your spouse typically need from you when they want to talk?

The overall goal is for you each to describe how the other can best meet your communication needs. Then both of you can work to communicate in the way that helps the other feel most supported.

Validate Your Spouse

"Anxiety weighs down the heart, but a kind word cheers it up" (Prov. 12:25). We've found that we feel cared for when our spouse immediately validates us with just a simple response before saying anything else. Validation is an essential aspect of your communication. Deepening your emotional communication and validating your spouse will have a vital impact on your relationship functioning and happiness.

Validation is when you clearly express understanding, acceptance, and support to your spouse. It's also acknowledging the legitimacy of your spouse's experiences, behaviors, emotions, wants, goals, thoughts, sensations, or actions. Keep in mind that fully accepting your spouse and acknowledging what they're saying doesn't necessarily mean you agree with their behaviors.

Consider some of the ways that expressing validating statements can strengthen your marriage. Communicating acceptance, empathy, and understanding will:

help you and your spouse feel heard, loved, understood, and supported;

regulate your emotions and help you cope;

lower your stress levels;

improve your mental health;

strengthen your relationship quality; and

nurture your sexual intimacy.[13]

Invalidation will harm your relationship and lower the chances you two will share your thoughts and emotions in the future. The opposite of validating is responding with criticism or rejection or discounting or disregarding their experiences, thoughts, emotions, or needs.[14] Not responding at all can also be invalidating to your spouse. Emotional intimacy grows out of a high level of trust from mutually sharing and receiving validation. When you express acceptance and empathy, you will become more aware of your spouse's needs and increase your intimacy.[15]

For the two of us, learning how to communicate has been a process. When our marriage was almost in shambles, Kristin learned in therapy how to ask for and accept validation. Here's a picture of the transformation of our conversations over the years. Notice how we now integrate both feelings and solutions along with validating one another.

Twelve years ago:

Kristin: It's been a really hard day. The nurse called out, and Bethany Grace has been getting sicker and sicker. It's been nonstop suctioning, oxygen, and cleaning up vomit. I'm so exhausted and just need a shower. I'm scared she's going to end up in the ER.

Todd: Okay . . . what do you want me to do about it? I've had a really stressful day at work, and I'm really hungry. What meds does she need right now?

Kristin steps back and looks away.

Kristin: Fine. You don't care. I'll go fix dinner.

Todd: You never believe that I care. You just think the worst of me!

Todd walks out of the room. Kristin emotionally shuts down. We don't talk the rest of the evening.

Two years later (following Kristin's work in therapy and striving to improve communication as a couple):

Kristin: I'm not doing well. I've had a really hard day. Bethany Grace has gotten sicker and sicker throughout the day. I'm scared she's going to end up in the ER.

Todd stands staring, not sure what he's supposed to do. He doesn't want to say the wrong thing and spark an argument.

Kristin: This is where I need you to say, "That sounds really hard. I'm sorry you've been caring for her nonstop and that you're worried that she's getting sicker."

Todd: Okay, thank you for telling me. That sounds really hard. I'm sorry you've had such a long day and that you're worried she's getting sicker.

Todd hugs Kristin.

Kristin: Thank you. That really means a lot. How was your day?

Todd: It's been a long day. I still have a lot to do to get ready for Sunday's sermon.

Kristin: I'm sorry. How can I help?

Present day:

Kristin: I've had a really hard day. The nurse called out, and Bethany Grace has been getting sicker and sicker all day. I haven't even had a break to take a shower. I'm scared she's going to end up in the ER.

Todd: I'm so sorry that you've had such a hard day. You must be exhausted. Yeah, I thought she didn't look good when I walked in the door. I can see why you're concerned. You go take a shower, and I'll start on dinner. Is there anything else I can do?

We hug.

Kristin: Thank you for validating me. I feel cared for. (*Kristin gives Todd a quick kiss.*) Maybe just watch her really closely. How was your day?

Todd: It's been very stressful. Two employees showed up late, and one of the vehicles had mechanical issues. I still have so much work to do.

Kristin: You have had a stressful day! I'm so sorry it hasn't gone well. I'll go take a quick shower and come out to finish fixing dinner so you can get some work done.

Todd: That will really help take some of the stress off. Thank you. Don't rush. Enjoy your shower.

We hug and kiss.

Kristin: I love you.

Todd: Love you too.

We've learned that it's important to normalize how the other person is feeling by saying things like, "It makes sense you're feeling that way with what you've been through." You both want to feel heard, understood, and accepted. It may feel like you shouldn't have to tell your spouse what you need them to say, but they can't possibly know what you're thinking and needing if you don't tell them. Sometimes we don't even know how we're feeling until we start talking about it. We also find it helpful to have a visual in front of us, like a list of emotions. These are easy to find online, or you might already have your child's emotions chart on the fridge. When you coach each other in what responses would be most meaningful for you, in the future your spouse will have a better idea of how to communicate they care for you.

Just repeating back what your spouse said may feel insincere. But if you are truly being genuine, it will mean a great deal to your spouse. Sharing thoughts and feelings will take practice. But over time, it will become more natural and greatly improve your communication and emotional connection. Be patient with one another and continue to talk openly.

Try responding with some of these validating phrases, which we have found to be powerful in the healing of our relationship:

"I'm sorry that you're going through this."

"I can see that you've worked really hard today!"

"It seems like you have a lot on you right now and are feeling stressed. How can I help?"

"That sounds like it was really hard."

"Would you like to talk about it?"

"Of course you're upset. I'd be upset too."

"You're doing a great job."

"You are an amazing parent."

"Sounds like you could use a break. I'll do that."

Think about what your spouse's current communication needs might be. Are they just looking for validation for their emotions? Do they need to share about their situation without being given advice? Would it be helpful to offer problem-solving suggestions or to just listen and provide emotional support? What's a statement that you think might help your spouse feel supported? *Hint: ask them instead of assuming you know what they need.*

Remember, you don't have to understand. You just need to communicate that you want to understand and that you believe in them and support them.

Give Your Spouse Feedback

Share with your spouse what's helpful and what's not helpful. Positively reinforce times they say and do things that make you feel cared for. Say something like, "Thank you for saying that. That helps me know you really care," or "It meant a lot to me when you . . ."

When your spouse does or says something unhelpful, instead of withdrawing (like Kristin used to), tell your spouse, "That hurt me when you . . ." Your spouse probably doesn't know how it made you feel. Both of you have to be willing to tell one another what you need and be willing to openly receive loving feedback. Really take the time to listen to one another and express acceptance and understanding despite the demands in your daily life. We believe you will be amazed at how this simple skill will strengthen your relationship.

8. Resolving Disagreements

Conflict is going to happen. It's safe to say that you are not going to agree on every issue. Couples facing significant challenges with their children are at greater risk for experiencing frequent, heated, and unresolved conflict.[16] On top of that, it will be challenging to find enough time to fight well and come to a resolution.

But when we avoid talking about stressful issues and conflict, the issues remain unresolved and resentment, division, and emotional distance will build.[17]

All couples argue, even happily married couples.[18] But there's a reason that some couples remain happily married while others grow apart. It's not that couples argue but *how* couples argue. Caregiving couples who enjoy higher marital quality use healthy conflict resolution strategies.[19] In his book *The Seven Principles for Making Marriage Work*, researcher John M. Gottman explains that happy couples accept they will always disagree on some issues, but they talk about their problems with a sense of humor.[20]

In *The Relationship Cure*, Gottman calls couples who have been able to argue without it damaging their relationship "marital masters." He says,

> [They] are so good at handling conflict that they make marital squabbles look like fun. It's not that these couples don't get mad and disagree. It's that when they disagree, they're able to stay connected and engaged with each other. Rather than becoming defensive and hurtful, they pepper their disputes with flashes of affection, intense interest, and mutual respect.[21]

In other words, healthy relationships have a combination of constructive conflict and high levels of intimacy. These couples also acknowledge that they will not be able to resolve all their relationship problems, and yet they still express that they love and accept one another.[22]

Over the years, we've learned that some issues just aren't worth spending time and energy fighting over. We have way too many big issues to waste time arguing about things that really won't matter in the long run. This means that both of us just let some things go when they aren't really important. We encourage you to pick your battles and spend as much time as you possibly can enjoying one another.

So, let's go through several different tools for effectively approaching arguments so you can grow as a couple as you face situational stressors and issues related to your child's complex needs. If you're fighting while trying to solve a situational problem, you can also refer to chapter 6.

Resolve Your Conflict Lovingly

When you do find yourselves in an argument, use this Scripture as your guide: "Love is patient and kind. Love is not jealous or boastful or proud or rude. It does not demand its own way. It is not irritable, and it keeps no record of being wronged" (1 Cor. 13:4–5 NLT). When tension is rising, we suggest that you each:

Stop and take three slow, deep breaths together.

Apologize if you've already done or said something hurtful.

Eat a snack or share a cup of tea or coffee while you begin talking.

Hold hands or touch your spouse's arm.

Invite God's Spirit into the conversation.

Mindfully Listen

As we mentioned in chapter 4, living mindfully is a powerful tool for handling stress—and that includes *listening* mindfully. Remember, to be mindful is to live fully in your present moment. When you're in a discussion with your spouse:

Put away all distractions (your phones, TV, etc.).

Give your full attention to your spouse.

Express interest (verbally and nonverbally).

Observe their facial expressions, emotions, and pain.

Listen without judging what they're saying.

Fully and unconditionally accept your spouse and what the situation is (this doesn't mean you necessarily agree with them or the situation).

Become aware of your own thoughts, emotions, and urges to say or do something.

Be fully accepting and nonjudgmental of yourself (this doesn't mean you agree with what you've done or said).

Stay in the present conversation. Avoid thinking about past arguments or worrying about the future.

Seek to Understand First

"Don't look out only for your own interests, but take an interest in others, too" (Phil. 2:4 NLT). Listen to your spouse to try to imagine where they're coming from and to learn what they want and need. Ask questions to better understand. Make sure your spouse feels heard. You may not agree with them, but they need to feel like you have listened and considered their thoughts and emotions. To ensure that you are understanding them, rephrase the essence of their statement and repeat it back to them by using one of these phrases:

"I can see . . ."

"It seems . . ."

"It sounds like . . ."

"I'm hearing you say _____. Is that correct?"

Put the Problem into Perspective

One strategy that has worked well for us is honestly sharing how important the issue is for each of us. Ask one another, "On a scale of 1 to 10, how important is this issue for you?" Both of you give a number (1 is "not important to me" and 10 is "extremely important to me"). If it's lower in importance for both of you, consider just dropping the issue. If it's higher, tell each other why.

If it's significantly higher for one of you, the other person might consider agreeing to go with their spouse's opinion, simply because it's really important to them.

Phrase Your Words Carefully

Thomas Gordon first introduced the idea of using "I statements" in his 1970 parenting book *Parent Effectiveness Training*.[23] By using "I feel . . ." and "I think . . ." statements, the speaker is not putting the listener on the defensive. Compare these two approaches to the same issue:

> Attacking: "You never listen to me. You always think you're right about what our daughter needs!"
> Effective: "I feel like when I try to share with you how I feel, I'm not always heard or understood."

Also, frame your "I statement" in the positive. Consider these two approaches:

> Attacking: "I can't believe you don't see that Bethany Grace needs to go back to OT."
> Effective: "I've noticed that Bethany Grace's fine motor skills seem to be weaker again. I think we need to take her for a new OT eval. I'd like to hear your thoughts."

In both examples, the first approach is attacking. The second way of phrasing the statement makes it less likely that the listener will react or feel criticized. The listener is also more likely to consider what their spouse is saying. Avoid extreme statements like:

"You always . . ."
"You never . . ."
"You just want . . ."

"I never get to . . ."

"I'm always the one . . ."

"There's no way that will work."

"That's the worst idea."

Final Tips for Going Deeper in Your Communication

Sharing a commitment to approaching your discussions with these ground rules in mind will draw you even closer:

Share how you feel. Communicate all of your feelings, including positive, neutral, and negative emotions. Speak up—directly ask for what you want and need.

Focus on the issue. Attack the dilemma together, not one another. Avoid blaming—you don't have the time or emotional energy for this. Face the problem as opposed to avoiding the real issues.

Be flexible. Stay open-minded. Move toward the middle ground and be willing to compromise. Let go of the need to be right or get your way.

Think the best of one another. Assume your spouse has good intentions and is doing their best.

Take a break. If the tension is escalating or you can't come to a resolution, agree to take a break. Do something to calm down such as deep breathing, exercising, or listening to music before resuming your conversation. By practicing a mindfulness exercise, you can reenter the conversation with lower anxiety, frustration, anger, and hostility.[24]

End the conversation positively. Apologize again for any hurtful statements or actions. Hug and kiss.

Remember: "Always be humble and gentle. Be patient with each other, making allowance for each other's faults because of your love" (Eph. 4:2 NLT).

Build the Skills

Step 1: Identify Where You Are

1. Think about the interactions you have with one another throughout a typical day, or think about the last two days. How many positive moments do you share? How many negative interactions do you experience? Describe these interactions.

Wife:

Positive

_____

_____

Negative

_____

_____

Husband:

Positive

_____

_____

Negative

_____

_____

2. Look at what conversations you typically have on a daily or weekly basis. Consider these eight types of conversations: Coordinating

Schedules, Chitchatting, Planning Together, Discussing Your Child's Needs, Problem-Solving, Checking In, Sharing Thoughts and Feelings, and Resolving Disagreements.

Which types most often take up your time?

_____

_____

3. Which types do you feel you are most effective at having as a couple?

_____

4. Which types would you like to become more skilled at as a couple?

_____

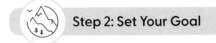 **Step 2: Set Your Goal**

1. How can you become more effective and efficient with the first five types of conversations to make time for deeper conversations?

_____

_____

2. Together, pick one conversation type you would like to improve upon in the coming week.

Conversation type: _____

3. Bonus goal: For one week, try starting each conversation by identifying if you need a "feelings" or a "solutions" conversation and communicate that to your spouse.

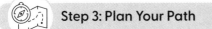 **Step 3: Plan Your Path**

List the specific ways you can strengthen your skills in that conversation type:

_____

_____

_____

Date you will take these steps by: _____

---------------------------------- **Pray Together** ----------------------------------

God, we know you are love. Fill us with you and teach us how to communicate our love for one another in more effective ways. Help us to grow closer and go deeper in our emotional connection. Give us more little moments we can enjoy together. Thank you for your amazing love and for how you are pulling us closer to you and to one another. In Jesus's name, amen.

6

Tackle Problems Together

Working to Creatively Solve Everyday Problems

And we know that God causes everything to work together for the good of those who love God.

Romans 8:28 NLT

Todd: I clearly remember the first time Kristin ever made me a sandwich, early in our relationship. It was such a loving act. But there was
no question about it, she did it completely wrong. The peanut butter to
jelly ratio was all off, and the bread didn't line up properly. She couldn't
actually expect me to eat a sandwich like that, and it was my duty to
tell her so. I began explaining the problems with the way she'd made
the sandwich. With each point, her face grew redder and redder. Then
she opened the peanut butter jar, grabbed a handful, and lunged at me.
I'll just say that the interaction ended with peanut butter up my nose
and in my ears. I learned an important lesson about problem-solving
and conflict that day: I'm not always right, and some problems are not
worth arguing over.

As we got further into our marriage, the problems got a lot more challenging. Misunderstandings about the proper way to make a sandwich paled in comparison to figuring out how to agree on the best ways to help our children. We had to learn better ways of working together. It's no secret that caregiving parents face significantly more stressful and complex issues than the average family. Remember all those sticky notes with your responsibilities from chapter 3? In addition to the endless tasks and time demands you already repacked in your bags, you may also have increased out-of-pocket costs for medical bills, specialty childcare, therapies, medications, special supplies, and/or loss of employment. As your problems accumulate, the stress intensifies. Not only do you have more taxing situations to discuss but you have less time and energy to talk and problem solve, and you are likely sleep deprived.

These intense strains can easily lead to conflicts in your marriage. Developing good problem-solving skills is especially important for disability parents to help lower stress levels.[1] If the two of you don't take the time to learn to deal with problems in effective ways, you might be destined for a life of peanut butter up your nose, or worse.

Strengthen Your Problem-Solving Skills

There is hope! It is very possible to find solutions to balancing your family's needs and demands. But you may need to take your collaborative problem-solving skills to the next level. To effectively problem solve together, you will also need to use your emotion-regulation skills from chapter 4 and your communication skills from chapter 5. Combine all three sets of skills, and you will be an unstoppable team.

All problems can be broken down into two parts. First, there is the situational dilemma causing stress in your life. You can identify the obstacle with a concrete statement like, "We don't have enough money to pay the rent this month." The second aspect of the problem is the emotional component that can elevate stress levels. Not having the money to pay rent may cause you to feel embarrassed or like a failure.

As there are two aspects to each problem, there are two predominant ways of coping with the stress in your lives. In chapter 4, we looked at the first approach, which is emotion-focused coping or emotion-regulation strategies. These skills help you get in a better frame of mind to tackle your problems. Beginning the problem-solving process in a regulated emotional state will help set you up to be more productive and successful together. Heightened emotions and feeling stressed can interfere with effective problem-solving.[2] Remember, if at any time during your problem-solving process you notice that your emotions are becoming intense, take a break and use one of the calming skills. Also talk about what emotions are coming up for you both.

In this chapter we are going to focus on the second approach, which is problem-focused coping. It is difficult to find a solution if you don't honor both the problem-focused and emotion-focused sides of the process. Problem-focused skills help you find a solution for how to change the situation to prevent recurring stress.[3] Obviously, you're not going to be able to prevent every problem. However, disability parents who use a problem-focused coping style are found to experience lower stress levels and greater well-being.[4] What's more, when a couple's problem-solving skills are like-minded and they work together as a team, they function better and enjoy a more fulfilling romantic relationship.[5]

Here are some other important pointers to keep in mind before you start tackling your problems together.

Remain Optimistic

When you approach obstacles with a hopeful outlook, you will be more effective at problem-solving, adapt more easily, take better care of yourself and your family, lower your stress, and be more resilient as a couple.[6] Pause for a moment to remind yourselves of this principle and approach the conversation with a positive and hopeful attitude.

Take Care of Your Physical Needs

We have a term in our house: "grumpy-hungry." Through many years of interactions, we've learned not to discuss difficult issues when we're hungry, as it never goes well. Our physical need for food distracts us from focusing on the problem, and we become irritable and short with one another the longer the conversation goes on. Other physical needs can prevent you from being able to concentrate on a problem. If one of you is extremely sleep deprived, if the work or caregiving day was more stressful than usual, or if your child needs something from you right then, it will be almost impossible to have a constructive conversation.

Once you've identified that there is a problem to be discussed, decide if there are physical needs that should be addressed before you both can focus on the issue at hand. It might be best to eat a snack, change a diaper, or take care of your child's immediate needs before diving into an intense discussion. You may even agree to talk about the problem the next day if the issue can wait. But with your family's busy schedule, it may feel like there's never a good time. There may not be, and you can't just keep postponing the conversation over and over. Ideally, wait until you both can really focus on the problem, but don't put the conversation off any longer than that. This balance will honor your relationship and the problem and will lead to a more productive problem-solving session.

Work as a Team

Problems can often divide us and make us feel isolated. Remember your commitment to one another. You're on the same team. You're working to solve this together for the good of your family and your marriage. Even if you have different thoughts about the problem, your goal is to improve your life together. You may disagree about the specific issue, but you'll find solidarity in your commitment to each other and to your family. This approach will help the problem-solving experience become a building, collaborative experience rather than a dividing one. We know that when we work together, there is almost nothing we can't solve!

Tackle Your Problems Together

Now that we've established our foundation, let's dig into the steps for tackling problems together.

Step 0: Decide if You Both Need to Solve the Problem

Some problems just don't require a joint decision. In fact, if you spent time discussing every problem, you would get bogged down and not get anything done. So, the beginning step is to determine whether one spouse can make the decision by themselves. If you're unsure, then of course discuss it together. If you just want to run your conclusions or decisions by each other to make sure you're in agreement, then do that. This will still save you time and emotional energy. It's probably easy for one spouse to make decisions for some tasks, like deciding what to cook for dinner or how to trim the hedges. What's harder is to allow and empower one spouse to make bigger decisions on their own for the family.

Todd: There was one month when a bill was due two days before my next paycheck, and we didn't have the money. Managing our finances was an area in which Kristin had empowered me to solely make decisions. So, without talking with her, I made a cash withdrawal on the credit card for the $300 that we were short. I decided the hefty fee was cheaper than not paying the larger bill. I didn't take this decision lightly, but I also didn't consult Kristin on it. It would have stressed her out and made it more difficult for her to focus on her responsibilities.

When either of us makes a decision like this, we feel the weight of that responsibility because we know our actions will impact each other and our family. We even make the wrong choice sometimes. But we have also committed to giving grace to one another and believing we are both doing our best. When things go wrong, we don't hold it against the other person.

By empowering and trusting one another, you can help relieve each other's burdens and get more done. As you learned when you redistributed your responsibilities in chapter 3, you need to divide and conquer many tasks. Giving that trust and letting go of control can be very challenging. Yet, by giving over control, you will free up your marriage to deal with bigger problems that really do take both of you to solve. When you do find a problem that needs you both, begin step 1 and continue down the path of problem-focused coping.

Step 1: Define the Problem

Perhaps you remember doing math word problems as a child. At first, the problem just felt overwhelming. The key was to translate all those sentences into smaller, manageable pieces you could use to find a solution. The first and most important step was to list all the facts and variables. To solve life's problems, you have to follow a similar process, but your "word" problems are much more advanced!

First, look at the situation and list everything you can pertaining to it. Since most of your problems are more complicated, you probably ought to write everything down. Let's look at an example problem: "I can't take our child to OT this week."

Though this is a short statement, it may actually be a very complicated problem. When you begin looking at all the factors, make sure to also share how you feel about the problem, not just practical variables. Your list might look something like this:

If we cancel, I'm worried that they may not let us keep coming.

Money is tight, and we can't afford it.

We have only one car, and you have to go to work.

Her brother has a doctor's appointment at the same time.

Last time she had a meltdown, and I just can't take that again.

As you look at the list together, you might realize that to solve this problem, you need to address a lot of smaller pieces first. By listing all the different issues, you can work on each little piece together using the next steps.

Step 2: Brainstorm Creative Solutions

As you address the smaller pieces, you may need to research, brainstorm, or ask other disability parents for ideas. One strategy that has helped our family through the years is having brainstorming sessions. We sit down as a couple or gather in the living room with our children or our parents, and everyone throws out ideas or asks questions to clarify the problem further. The only rules are you can't negate or debate. This time is solely dedicated to getting the creative juices flowing. So, with the OT dilemma, the two of you might throw out ideas like:

Ask if you can reschedule.

Call a rideshare.

Ask family or friends if they can take your child to OT.

Check with churches about transportation ministries or financial help.

Research state or other organizations that may offer medical transportation.

Consider asking a coworker to pick you up for work.

Decide if you could ride your bike to work.

Ask the therapy center about a payment plan.

There are no bad ideas, even though some may seem far out there. Your job is to be open-minded and come up with as many new and creative ideas as possible. A good rule of thumb during this process is to start every statement with "Yes, and . . ." This will validate the previous statement and help create a collaborative experience. This process can actually be a lot of fun and help relieve some of the stress of the situation. Approach this time with an appropriate balance of lightheartedness and seriousness.

When the kids were young, we just couldn't make all the finances work on a month-to-month basis with Kristin staying home as a full-time caregiver. Desperate solutions that we considered included going into debt, declaring bankruptcy, or taking out a second mortgage on the house. We don't recommend any of those. Thankfully, after a lot of creative thinking, we discovered we could use our credit card rewards to help pay some of our mortgage each month. We also became extreme couponers and saved thousands a year on our everyday needs. We encourage you to think outside the box and find unique ways to solve your problems.

Step 3: Identify Your Resources

Over the years, we've learned about free resources, mostly from other caregiving parents. In the resources section, we list organizations that provide assistance to families with disabilities. If you're not already familiar with these programs, make sure to look into them. Most of these resources are free to all, but some are based on income level and depend on your state. Every little bit of help relieves some pressure and frees up your time and funds for needed items. Your local resources might include respite care programs, home modification services, equipment exchange programs, different church ministries, medication assistance programs at children's hospitals, school system advocates, and disability lawyers. Also, refer to step 3 in chapter 3 for additional local resource ideas.

State programs typically provide early intervention services, school services (starting at age three), medical cost assistance programs, respite care grants, Medicaid and Medicaid waivers, home health care and the Katie Beckett Waiver, medical transportation, and resources through the Department of Intellectual and Developmental Disabilities. Social Security Disability Income is the major federal program and is based on income and disability conditions. Nationwide resources include medication assistance programs (through the drug companies, and ask at pharmacies as well), parent training organizations, and free recreational programs such as Special Olympics.

Step 4: Together Decide on a Plan

Take all those ideas from your brainstorming session and resources and see what makes the most sense to solve your unique problem. It may take more than one solution to make the situation work. For example, a friend may take your child to OT, a coworker may pick up your spouse, and you may drive your other child to their doctor's appointment. One of the biggest criteria you will use to determine your plan is to look at your priorities that you set in chapter 3.

Next, look at your strengths and weaknesses and decide both as a couple and individually if you can follow through on this plan. For example, we had a major problem when Bethany Grace kept chewing through her feeding tube line every night. We brainstormed a solution that combined Todd's engineering skills and Grammy's sewing skills to make a reloadable, quilted sleeve that Bethany Grace couldn't chew through. That idea utilized their strengths to solve a problem and left Kristin free to work on other issues that she was better equipped to handle.

Most solutions are probably going to mean that one or both of you will need to change your plans, schedules, or roles. If you aren't willing to sacrifice, either the problem isn't going to get solved or one of you is going to begrudgingly do it, which isn't good for anyone. You may also have to come up with a brand-new idea for which neither of you has experience. Be flexible and decide to give that new idea a try. Approaching this time with open minds and selflessness will make it much easier to come to an agreeable and workable solution.

Finally, you might conclude that you haven't found a good plan. In that case, go back to brainstorming again—right then if you have time, or sometime soon if you need to take care of other things first. You might try more ways to find outside help. Type your problem into a search browser, do some AI queries to get a different perspective, or look up special needs blogs or videos that might give hacks and tips for your unique problem. There are lots of resources out there. It's crucial to include them in your problem-solving process.

Step 5: Put Your Plan into Action

Once you have your plan, it's time to get started on it. One of you will likely be taking the lead, but that doesn't mean the other person isn't a part of the process. While one partner is implementing steps, the other can assume a support role. Along the way, the supporting partner can ask, "How can I help you?" and follow through on their spouse's answer. You can also jump in and start helping in ways you know you can. Try giving words of encouragement and tell them that they're doing a great job or that you've really noticed a difference because of their efforts. Thank them for their time and leadership in that area. Find other ways to be supportive and let your spouse know you care for and value them.

Step 6: Reevaluate

Not every solution is going to work perfectly. If your problem hasn't been solved, it's time to go back through the problem-solving process. Keep trying different ideas until you find one that works. The key is to persevere together and not let the challenge bring you down or come between you.

Rely on God

Inevitably, sometimes you will come up short and realize your own limitations. You can't solve every issue. So, give all your anxiety and worries to God. Pray and ask him for what you need, and he will come through in ways you could never imagine. We can't tell you how many times we were trying to figure out how to pay a bill when someone came up to us and handed us money. One time a church member stopped by and said, "Here's $174," which was exactly what we needed to make ends meet that month. We remember times that were so rough we could barely function, and our church brought us meals for weeks straight. Their support and the gift of saving us so much time kept us going.

We encourage you to "not be anxious about anything, but in every situation, by prayer and petition, with thanksgiving, present your requests to God. And the peace of God, which transcends all understanding, will guard your hearts and your minds in Christ Jesus" (Phil. 4:6–7).

Build the Skills

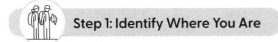 **Step 1: Identify Where You Are**

Think of a problem the two of you are currently facing that you need to tackle together.

Define the problem:

_____

_____

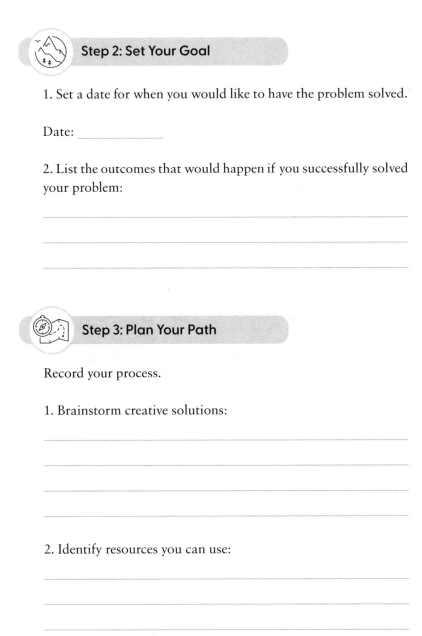

Step 2: Set Your Goal

1. Set a date for when you would like to have the problem solved.

Date: _____

2. List the outcomes that would happen if you successfully solved your problem:

_____

_____

_____

Step 3: Plan Your Path

Record your process.

1. Brainstorm creative solutions:

_____

_____

_____

_____

2. Identify resources you can use:

_____

_____

_____

_____

3. Together, decide on a plan and list the steps:

Pray Together

God, we know that nothing is impossible with you! You will always make a way as we seek after your wisdom and guidance. We know you cause "all things to work together for good to those who love [you]" (Rom. 8:28 NASB). Help us to trust you more. Give us wisdom and inspiration to look at our problems and patience with one another as we work on solutions together. We thank you for your goodness and provision in our lives, and we want to lean on you more every day. In Jesus's name, amen.

7

Find Shelter in One Another

Moving through Grief and Chronic Sorrow

The Lord is close to the brokenhearted; he rescues those whose spirits are crushed.

Psalm 34:18 NLT

At thirty weeks pregnant with our second child, we gripped hands in the geneticist's office. We held our breath as the doctor delivered the devastating news that if Bethany Grace survived, she would be born with a severe chromosomal deletion called Cri du Chat Syndrome. We listened to the prognosis that she would likely never walk or talk, be severely intellectually disabled, and have any number of medical problems, including heart defects. The doctor's declaration sent shock waves through our bodies. We went home and lay in bed, holding each other and sobbing all night long. We shared our excruciating disappointment, anguish, and loss. Our dreams of having a healthy daughter had been shattered. All we had was each other.

We supported one another through this period of acute grief, but the following months and years of our chronic sorrow nearly tore our marriage apart. We eventually learned that working through grief as a couple is an ongoing process. Sharing grief can be challenging, but developing this skill is critical for growing a strong marriage while caring for a child with disabilities.

Recognize Your Acute Grief

When couples first realize the implications of their child's condition or diagnosis, the emotional pain that they feel is called acute grief.[1] Many parents react strongly, and this initial time period can be traumatic and overwhelming.[2] You may have gone through this first grief period years ago—at your child's birth, at three years old, after you adopted them, when they endured a traumatic injury, or when they showed signs of regression or other symptoms later in life. You may feel like your child has been taken from you. Or your grief experience may not fit into any of these descriptions. You may even be walking through this dark season of acute grief right now. Every special needs parenting couple has a unique grief story. For us, we were mourning for our daughter who never was. For over half of the pregnancy, we had imagined what Bethany Grace would be like before we learned about her severe genetic syndrome. This type of grief can feel ambiguous for parents, because the loss is not of an actual child but rather of the child for whom they were hoping and expecting.[3]

Journey through Chronic Sorrow

We couldn't have fathomed how complicated the grieving process is for parents of children with chronic illnesses and disabilities. We believed that once we grieved this crushing diagnosis, we would begin to fully accept our daughter and our new life. We didn't understand that parents of children with special needs experience a different type of long-term grief process in addition to the period of acute grief. People often think about moving through the classic five stages of grief.[4] But this model doesn't fit the grieving process for disability parents, who experience a unique, ongoing, and cyclical grief process.[5] You see, after the intense period of acute shock and grief, the journey of chronic sorrow begins.[6] We didn't realize that our grief journey had just begun with the diagnosis, and that it would continue throughout Bethany Grace's life. No one explained this to us. We didn't know how to navigate this painful journey or understand what was happening inside our spouse or what this disconnect was doing to our marriage.

For caregiving parents, mourning reemerges when we experience smaller or new losses. Throughout your child's life, there may be no definite end to the triggers that will reactivate your grief. Different events may cause emotional pain for one or both of you. Triggers typically include developmental milestones, the start of a new school year, your child's birthday, medical events, or a worsening in your child's condition. You might feel sadness or other strong emotions while shopping for toys for your child that are on a much lower developmental level, seeing another child similar in age, or responding to a person staring or asking questions. There might even be daily reminders that cause new pangs of sadness. Your grief is not sequential. Rather, it's an unpredictable and continual process.[7] Some describe this journey as a "living loss."[8]

Understand the States of Grief and Chronic Sorrow

Disability parents cycle through different emotional states of grief during acute grief and on their journey of chronic sorrow. There are five major emotional states you will likely move through from time to time: shock and denial, anger, anxiety and fear, sadness or depression, and guilt.[9] There is no formula to the process, and you can be in more than one state at a time. New events or thoughts

117

can cause you to experience the same emotional state again. Different emotions may affect you simultaneously or at times that don't make sense to you. You may not experience the same states of grief at the same time as your spouse. This can be difficult to recognize, frustrating, and hard to understand.[10] Problems can arise if one or both of you become stuck in a state.

Let's look at how each state can impact your relationship, how you can process those emotions in a healthy way, and ways you can also support one another.

Shock and Denial

When you first noticed your child's symptoms or received their diagnosis, you might have felt emotionally numb, like it wasn't real. You may also have experienced disbelief and physical symptoms, such as an inability to sleep or changes in appetite. Though your reactions may have seemed similar to one another's, there were likely also differences in your experiences. Every individual responds to this type of life-altering news in very personal ways. Even before hearing the doctor speak the official diagnosis, you may have already known, but one or both of you were in denial. This could cause conflict between you.

Kristin once counseled a couple seeking marital support after receiving their son's autism spectrum disorder (ASD) diagnosis. The mother was desperate to do anything to help her child. The father, on the other hand, was still in denial and was not supporting his wife or acknowledging her concerns. And so conflict festered, and they became less connected. After weeks of counseling and intentionally seeking to understand each other's reactions to grief, the parents learned how to better support one another emotionally and to partner in parenting their son. They realized that they both loved their son and wanted the best for him, but were experiencing the difficulty and pain in very different ways.

Often mothers are first to see the early signs of their child's special needs and seek diagnosis on their own, as the father remains in denial.[11] If one spouse feels like their partner is dismissing their concerns, resentment can grow. To avoid resentment and move out of shock and denial, you have to allow yourselves to feel all the emotions surrounding the implications of your child's diagnosis or condition. Be patient and extend grace to each other during this painful period. No parent is ever fully prepared to hear heart-shattering news about their child's health or development. But also keep gently nudging each other to acknowledge your emotions and respond to the other person's and your child's needs. Throughout your child's life, new care needs, symptoms, or conditions may develop, and one or both of you may experience denial. You will need to work through this grief process together each time.

Anger

Anger can boil up from the intense pain and loss. You can feel anger toward the medical professionals or toward your family and friends who have "normal" lives. You may be directing anger inward, blaming yourself for your child's condition or the situation. You can even feel angry at your child. Often our spouse is the target of our anger. Anger is a secondary emotion, which means that below the surface a painful primary emotion is fueling this reaction. Some primary emotions include sadness, frustration, fear, guilt, embarrassment, jealousy, invalidation, and disappointment. To reduce your anger, you must first identify the root emotion causing you to feel angry.

For example, Kristin often expressed anger at Todd for not seeming to be as affected emotionally by Bethany Grace's medical needs. The root of her anger was embarrassment. She believed she shouldn't be feeling sad or overwhelmed, so she became angry at herself and angry at Todd because she felt inadequate.

Targeting your displaced anger at your spouse can block communication and create conflict. It's important to not automatically take your spouse's emotions personally or assume they're upset with you. Avoid taking your pain out on one another or blaming each other. Blaming prevents you from moving forward together and will not change anything that has already happened. Remember: you're both really hurting. Help each other identify the root emotions causing your anger so you can address the source and move through the grieving process together.

Anxiety and Fear

Anxious responses to grief can strain your marriage, especially when you're having difficulty understanding one another's reactions.

Kristin: Anxiety took control of my mind. I lived in a constant state of worry about Bethany Grace's health and future. I was reliving the traumatic moments of learning about her condition. I couldn't think clearly enough to talk about it to Todd. He didn't understand why I was so worried all the time. It didn't make sense to me that he wasn't worried.

Anxiety may manifest as worry, restlessness, or hypervigilance. One or both of you may feel inadequate or experience physical manifestations such as poor concentration, heart palpitations, racing thoughts, and inability to sleep. Anxiety can fuel your fears—fears of the future and the unknown, especially if your child's diagnosis is unclear and the prognosis uncertain. Anxiety-provoking questions like these might run through your mind:

How long will our child live?
Will our child be able to live independently someday?
How will we be able to provide for our child?
How will our child's high needs affect our other child(ren)?
Who will care for our child if something happens to us?

You may also live in a constant state of anxiety thinking about how the school might call about your child's problematic behaviors or that at any moment you may need to rush your medically complex child to the emergency room. To calm your anxiety, first validate your worries. It makes sense that you are anxious about these real possibilities and future unknowns. Give a voice to each other's uneasy thoughts. You may notice the signs of anxiety in your spouse before they are even aware. Encourage your spouse to process their worries and fears with you.

Work together to do what you can to prepare for or prevent these possible stressful situations. Learn as much specific information as you can regarding your child's condition and needed interventions. Talking with other caregiving parents and asking professionals questions might help relieve some of your fears. As you can, plan together for your child's future in practical ways.

When you've done what you can right now to take care of your child, continuing to worry about the future becomes unhealthy. The goal is to balance your stress of preparing for the future with living in the present moment. When you focus on what is right in front of you, not what might happen, your anxiety lowers. As you engage and process your anxieties, we also encourage you to try to give your worries to God and remember "he cares for you" (1 Pet. 5:7).

Sadness

Knowing that feeling ongoing sadness is a normal part of the mourning process can help you sympathize with one another. Waves of sorrow and heartache can overcome you at any time. It may seem like you get hit by despair out of nowhere and feel helpless. Other times you may know what caused your grief to resurface. The two of you will likely experience waves of grief at differing times from one another.

During your initial period of mourning, the sadness may last for weeks, and this is expected. Sorrow may also come and go after that. Sadness may also mix with other emotions such as joy and gratitude. This can feel confusing. Allow yourself to cry and experience all the different emotions. To be able to feel pleasant emotions, you have to allow yourself to feel the painful ones too.

Support your spouse by helping them feel safe coming to you in their sadness and uncertainty. Communicate that you would like to understand how they are feeling and that you recognize their emotional ups and downs are expected. You may feel like managing your own sadness leaves you no emotional energy to support your spouse. But you don't have to provide answers, and you cannot fix their pain. Simply be there for one another and fully accept each other in your uncomfortable and messy emotional states.

Guilt

Caregiving parents often carry heavy guilt and self-blame. This is typical but can be very unhealthy and increase psychological distress.[12] These feelings of guilt and shame might cause you to want to hide your thoughts from one another, which can create distance between you. Many disability parents can become stuck in replaying shaming thoughts and questions like the ones below.

Guilt for your child's condition.

I should've taken better care of myself during the pregnancy.

If only I'd been watching my child more closely, they wouldn't have had the accident.

If we'd begun interventions earlier, their delays might not be this severe.

Guilt about your marriage.

I should've listened to my spouse and taken our child for an evaluation sooner.

I haven't supported my spouse emotionally in their grief.

I assumed my spouse didn't care.

Guilt and shame about your thoughts.

Would it be better if our child hadn't survived?

What would people think if they knew what I was thinking?

I'm a horrible parent for feeling disappointed and just wanting a healthy child.

In the days following the devastating news about Bethany Grace, we began to avoid talking to one another. We were both horrified by the thoughts and feelings that were inside of us. Then one of us finally said what we had both been thinking, "Would it be better if Bethany Grace doesn't survive?" We were both relieved that the other person had been wrestling with similar thoughts and emotions.

We want you to know that what you're each thinking and feeling is normal. It's typical and painful to wonder what life would be like under different circumstances. If you've had these thoughts, we guarantee that you're not alone. It's more common than you might think. But guilt and shame can cause you to isolate and fear what your spouse might think of you if you share how you really feel. You need to keep talking to one another about your painful thoughts. It's vital you resolve your guilty feelings together. You may find that you both have been having similar thoughts. Reducing your self-blame and guilt will help you adapt easier and feel less despair.[13] In most cases, to move on from guilt, you need to extend yourselves compassion.

Here's an example of how you can rephrase your self-talk:

Guilt: "We should have seen that our child was showing these symptoms and done something sooner."

Self-compassion: "We didn't know, and we made the best possible decision at the time."

To heal and move past guilt and shame, extend compassion to yourself and to each other. Also gently remind your spouse to extend themselves compassion. Remember, your circumstances with your child are extraordinarily difficult and painful. It's expected that the two of you experience differing strong emotions and various thoughts.

Recognize Your Different Reactions

As you move among the five states of grief on your journey of chronic sorrow, expect to shift in and out of feelings of shock and denial, anger, anxiety and fear, sadness, and guilt. It's similar to a dance—allow yourself to move with your emotions while also keeping your focus right on your partner and your day in front of you. Welcome positive emotions as well, such as joy and gratitude for your relationship with your child and each other. And remember that each of you is likely moving through these emotions at a rhythm different from the other.

Todd: My amazing wife and our fragile daughter had finally come home from the NICU. But life began spinning out of control. It was all I could do to help change the feeding bag, monitor Bethany Grace's vitals, and fix a meal, much less try to somehow do my job. Kristin tried to talk to me when I got home from work, and I truly did try to listen. But it was more than I could handle. I didn't have the time or energy to deal with grief or other feelings. I had to take care of my family, or we were going to fall apart.

Kristin: It was all I could do to make it through the day without breaking down. Hearing Bethany Grace cry in pain frazzled my nerves. Sitting through appointment after disappointing specialist appointment made me even sadder. If I saw a pregnant woman or a healthy baby, panic and heartache crashed over me. Todd seemed to be past grieving and was unaffected by all the daily painful events. He just couldn't understand what I was going through. A couple of times I tried to tell him how I felt, but he said that I just needed to get over it and move on. I shut down and withdrew deep inside myself somewhere. I began to believe something was wrong with me, because I couldn't get over my grief and move on like he had. He hurt me. Deeply. I couldn't stand to be around him, much less let him touch me. I didn't see how our marriage was going to come back from this and survive.

Todd: Looking back, I know that in an effort to make sure we survived, I hurt people, especially Kristin. I ignored things and avoided my own feelings. I rationalized that there was no time for that. Perhaps that was true for a short time. But as the weeks stretched into months, and months became a year, it finally dawned on me that I was just living in crisis mode. No matter how hard I worked, I couldn't change the situation. The demands would still be there every day. The outlook would remain mostly the same. If I didn't slow down and engage with my feelings, our family really would break—not because of our daughter but because of me.

As time passed, our reactions and grief paths diverged. This is not uncommon for couples. The grief that disability parents experience is complicated and intense. Now add each spouse's differences in personality and your own process, and navigating this season together can be very challenging. Each of you may feel like you're on a completely different grief journey. This can create hurt, distance, and a breakdown in communication.

You will likely experience different emotional reactions to the same events. That doesn't mean one of your experiences is right and the other person's is invalid. You're coming into this difficult situation with very different life experiences and perhaps even histories of trauma, and it's expected that you might respond differently.

As you navigate your different emotional reactions, remember that you are not experiencing the exact same challenging circumstances on a day-to-day basis. Mothers often experience more intense chronic sorrow in comparison to fathers, for example.[14] Throughout their child's life, developmental milestones often trigger a wave of grief in the mother that is less intense for the father. While fathers often resign themselves to the diagnosis and experience a decrease in strong emotions over time, chronic sorrow can remain more permanent for some mothers.[15] Oftentimes, this is because the mother may be the primary caregiver and service coordinator.[16] She may be the one most often going to the doctors' and therapy appointments, managing challenging behaviors, caregiving at home, and being present for medical emergencies.[17] In other words, she's surrounded all day by the factors triggering grief and stress, which naturally strains her emotionally. The mother may also continue to have a harder time adapting because of her difficult experience during the pregnancy and childbirth.[18]

Spouses may also deal with their emotions differently. For example, a wife's coping style may be more emotion-focused, and a husband may detach from his emotions. Men often experience emotional inhibition and have a more difficult time expressing their feelings and crying. The husband may cope by becoming more action-oriented, focusing on problem-solving, and shifting to the stress of providing for his family and taking care of practical and financial matters.[19] This can lead to an unhealthy avoidance of processing intense emotions. As one wife told us, "My husband has a difficult time talking about his emotions. He's really quiet like that. But it builds up until he either breaks down or blows up." We've come to use the analogy of a volcano for when Todd allows his stress and emotions to build without talking about them. Differences in coping can create intense strain on the relationship. Yet, when couples learn to be interested in why their spouse is responding so differently, they can begin to better appreciate their spouse's circumstances, validate their experiences, and offer and receive emotional support.

Process Your Grief Individually and Together

Your Personal Grief

To move forward, each of you must move through your own personal grief, realize your emotions are expected, and be willing to experience your process of grieving. Your personal process will be unique and will not look like anyone else's. Moving through your grief means that you recognize the image you had for your child needs to be adapted to who your child actually is.[20] Talking with others about your loss and disappointment can help you move toward acceptance.[21] Healthy ways to process your grief include:

Attending a caregiver support group.

Talking to a friend or family member.

Praying and reading Scripture.

Joining a small group Bible study.

Journaling your thoughts and emotions.

Meeting with a pastoral counselor.

Seeing a professional therapist (especially if you are having difficulty grieving or are experiencing symptoms of trauma, depression, or anxiety).

Your Grief Together

Ultimately, for the health of your marriage, it's necessary to find a way to regularly and fully share your thoughts with one another and support one another emotionally. Distance will grow between you if one or both of you try to deal with your grief on your own. Feeling safe to share your painful thoughts and emotions with one another will draw you closer together. But it can be hard to be vulnerable, to talk and cry together. Here are some reasons couples might avoid grieving together:

Not wanting to experience the painful emotions.

Assuming your spouse might not feel the same way.

Feeling embarrassed.

Not wanting to burden your spouse or bring them down.

Lacking quality time to talk or not wishing to use your precious time that way.

Fearing you will be misunderstood or invalidated by your spouse.

Despite these obstacles, you have to include one another in your personal process. The deeper you can go, the greater your inner strength will be. Whatever you do, just keep talking about it. Keep a box of tissues handy and don't resist needing it. You may not feel like you have the strength to process your painful emotions together. Invite God into your grieving process. Allow him to counsel and comfort the two of you. If you can't find words, just hug and cry. Whisper a prayer asking God for help and strength and receive his peace. "And the Holy Spirit helps us in our weakness. For example, we don't know what God wants us to pray for. But the Holy Spirit prays for us with groanings that cannot be expressed in words" (Rom. 8:26 NLT).

As a couple, you share many losses that only the two of you can fully comprehend. You are also experiencing different individual losses that may be difficult for the other spouse to understand. But you still share the same loss of a healthy or neurotypical child. You also may be in different states of grief. One of you may be in denial, the other in sadness or anger. One or both of you may be struggling with spiritual doubts or clinical mental health symptoms. It's critical to validate one another's experiences and emotions and accept the ways the other grieves. Give one another grace and think the best of one another. The goal is to learn how to support each other even if you don't fully understand what your spouse is going through.

Your process as a couple will be special to your relationship's needs. When you open up to one another, you will not only allow yourselves to process your painful emotions but also share a special intimacy that's not possible any other way. Think about your spouse. What do you know about their losses and triggers? If anyone can understand their grief, it's you. You have the opportunity to love each other in a way other couples never experience. You are a gift to your spouse. No one else's grief journey will be like your spouse's, and no one else can support them through this like you can. Though your personal experiences are very different, you are on the same journey. And it's not an easy one. That's why you need one another more than ever. If you embrace this opportunity, you can walk together, united, and grow even closer in the process. Along the way, you can find shelter in one another and make your relationship a refuge from the storm.

Pray through Your Spiritual Struggles

Special needs parents often experience spiritual struggles as part of their grief process.[22] We can feel guilty and shameful for experiencing spiritual questioning and doubts or even anger or bitterness toward God. It's not uncommon to feel confused, abandoned, or punished by God. Many parents wrestle with questions like these:

How could God be good and allow our child to suffer?
Did we do something to deserve this pain and suffering?
Why did this have to happen to us?

We believe that disability parents sometimes hold back and don't admit their hard questions to themselves, their spouses, others, or God, because they believe to do so would be sinning. Yet, when we turn to Scripture, we see many examples of God's followers crying out to him in honest questioning. Take Job, for example. He endured unbearable suffering and loss. Essentially his sons and daughters were all killed, and he lost his entire business and livelihood. Job grieved and poured out his heart. "Therefore I will not keep silent; I will speak out in the anguish of my spirit, I will complain in the bitterness of my soul" (Job 7:11). He didn't curse God even though his wife told him to. But he did pour out his honest feelings and questions, and "In all this, Job did not sin by charging God with wrongdoing" (1:22).

God already knows your deepest, darkest, most shameful thoughts. David wrote, "O Lord, you have examined my heart and know everything about me. . . . You know what I am going to say even before I say it, Lord" (Ps. 139:1, 4 NLT). If anything, denying our thoughts and avoiding God will keep us in darkness and distance us more from God and from our spouse. Remember, "Even if we feel guilty, God is greater than our feelings, and he knows everything" (1 John 3:20 NLT).

Spiritual struggles can tear us apart. We have to be willing to openly talk about them with God and our spouse. Cry out to God together with your hurt, disappointment, and confusion. Ask for and be willing to receive his powerful counsel and healing.

Build the Skills

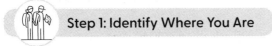 **Step 1: Identify Where You Are**

1. When did you experience your acute grief? Are you still in that season?

Wife:

Husband:

_____

_____

As a couple:

_____

_____

2. Identify your personal chronic sorrow triggers.

Wife:

_____

_____

Husband:

_____

_____

3. How do you experience the different states of grief in your chronic sorrow? Describe what each emotion looks like for you. Think about how you feel inside your body, your thoughts, your actions, things you might say, and urges you have. Then share your responses with each other.

Wife:

Shock/denial _____

Anger _____

Anxiety _____

Sadness _____

Guilt _____

Husband:

Shock/denial _____

Anger _____

Anxiety _____

Sadness _____

Guilt _____

4. How have you grieved in healthy ways?

Wife:

_____

_____

Husband:

_____

_____

As a couple:

_____

_____

5. Describe the barriers to sharing your journey of grief and chronic sorrow. What are some reasons you avoid talking to one another about your pain and loss?

Wife:

_____

_____

Husband:

_____

_____

6. How have you felt supported by your spouse as you struggle with chronic sorrow?

Wife:

_____

_____

Husband:

_____

_____

7. In what state(s) of chronic sorrow do you feel you are currently?

Wife:

_____

_____

Husband:

_____

_____

Step 2: Set Your Goal

1. What are some ways you can continue to process your own grief?

Wife:

Husband:

2. What are the potential steps you need to take to be able to move through your grief as a couple?

3. How can you best support your spouse in their grief journey?

Wife:

Husband:

4. **Pick one** action step from question 1, 2, or 3 to work on in the coming month.

Wife: _____

Husband: _____

Step 3: Plan Your Path

How will you implement the goal you chose?

Wife:

_____

_____

Husband:

_____

_____

Pray Together

God, our hearts are hurting. We're filled with so many different painful emotions. Our loss and grief can feel overwhelming at times. Holy Spirit, pray for us when we don't have the strength or the words. Please comfort us and heal our marriage. Draw us closer together as we share our loss and chronic sorrow. Thank you for your help and love. In Jesus's name, amen.

8

Stop to Rest Together

Prioritizing Respite Time Together

> Come, my beloved, let us go to the countryside, let us
> spend the night in the villages.
>
> Song of Songs 7:11

Kristin: When Todd and I first started backpacking together, I quickly realized that having him as a hiking partner was not going to be fun. His philosophy about the trail was the opposite of mine. He liked to push through at a fast pace, barely stopping to rest. If I asked about getting off the trail to go down to the creek or to a mountain overlook, his response was, "I want to get to the campsite. We can rest and enjoy ourselves there by the water." But by the time we finally stopped for the day and set up camp, I'd collapse, exhausted, because I hadn't had a chance to rest all day. So, I ended up not enjoying myself even at the campsite. The next morning, I'd begin the day already tired and burned out about the trip.

Over the years, we've learned to compromise when we hike. Todd is now willing to slow down, joke, laugh, and take the occasional detour off the trail to eat lunch by the creek. Kristin is willing to go longer between breaks and keep up the pace as best she can. But we've both learned that we enjoy the trip more, and we come back more rested, if we pace ourselves and stop for regular breaks. We've also discovered that we need to insert moments of fun and seeing new places along the path.

The Effects of Burnout

In your lives as a caregiving couple, are you just pushing on day in and day out without stopping to rest and enjoy life along the way? The additional caregiving needs, challenging behaviors, financial burdens, hospitalizations, and appointments equal less time as a couple. And the time that you do have to spend together, you may need to spend problem-solving with little opportunity left over to share your thoughts and emotions or have fun together. As a result, staying happy and close can feel like a constant battle. Many couples collapse exhausted at night and wake up tired the next morning. We can quickly get burned out, irritable, injured, and sick.

Disability parents, both mothers and fathers, experience a significantly higher rate of burnout than parents of children without special needs, with mothers experiencing a higher rate of burnout than fathers.[1] Burnout occurs due to a long period of caregiving and emotional stress. As opposed to an acute mental health crisis, burnout is a psychological reaction to long-term emotional strain. Results of burnout can include physical exhaustion, emotional fatigue, and psychological and cognitive symptoms.[2] If you keep pushing through the daily caregiving stress without regularly resting together, your emotional energy and connection with one another will drain.

Quality Time at Home

Stopping to rest together helps recharge your relationship. It's crucial to take breaks together to rest mentally, emotionally, physically, and spiritually. You have to talk and laugh throughout the day, get off the trail to see a different view, and stop to relax together. Getting out of the house for a short date night is like holding hands while wading in a creek or kissing at a mountain view. Escaping for a private night away is like running off the trail to skinny dip in a secluded waterfall lagoon.

Some caregiving couples have found that it helps to have a romantic meal together at home as often as they can, even if their children are with them.[3] This would be the time to give your child their favorite electronic device and not feel guilty about it. Sometimes we've been successful at just sitting at the kitchen table talking or snuggling and watching a movie together in the living room while Bethany Grace enjoys watching her tablet. You can also try setting a weekly date night to watch a movie in bed after the kids have gone to sleep. But the interruptions of screaming children, medical machines beeping, or needing to focus on feeding your child may not be conducive to spending quality time together.

Time at home can help build your relationship, but it's not enough. You also need time together away from your home and responsibilities.

The Value of Respite Care

Disability parents who have been successful in strengthening their marriages put their relationship first. They seek support so they can spend more time together and increase their intimacy and commitment to one another.[4] When disability parenting couples receive even short respite breaks, they experience improvement in their

stress levels
marriage relationship
family functioning
mental health

parenting effectiveness

optimism about their marriage and caring for their child[5]

When you're just trying to get through the stress of the day, it can be difficult to be fully present with one another. Breaks together outside the home can calm your physical stress responses and give you time to relax, rejuvenate, have fun, and just sit and talk. Having time to be mindful together—being fully present, engaged, and relaxed—promotes intimacy and can help you stay more connected in future difficult situations.[6] This time can also help you comfort one another and grow closer. Planning your getaway will give you a shared goal and something special to look forward to. When you come home from your time away, your stress levels will be lower, and you will be even better parents than you already were. You will also share a fun memory.

Neglecting getting away for time alone together grew to be a major factor in the decline of our marriage. Our relationship had deteriorated into a business partnership with our conversations consisting of, "What doctors' and therapy appointments do the kids have today?" "What time does the nurse leave?" "What time will you be home from work?" "What do we need from the store?" We hadn't made it a priority to find a way to enjoy time together outside of the house. This led to us not enjoying time together even at home. We had stopped joking, hugging, or kissing. So, how did we go from a barebones task-oriented relationship back to a thriving romance?

Kristin's psychiatrist gave us one of the best pieces of marriage advice we've ever received. At Kristin's lowest point, he proclaimed, "If the two of you don't find a way to get away together, it's not going to end well."

Four and a half years after Bethany Grace was born, we finally made the plunge and got away on a trip together. It took coordinating three grandparents and private-duty nursing, but we got away for a couple of nights. Bethany Grace was even a little sick, but we had to get away. We knew if our marriage was going to survive, we couldn't wait any longer. Taking that trip was one of the best steps we've ever taken for our marriage. We had an amazing time together, it motivated us to invest in our relationship, and we realized the importance of getting away with just the two of us.

Having plans in place to get away together has also greatly helped us psychologically over the years. When we first moved back to Nashville, another parent told us about a Saturday respite program at a local church. The program was only three hours once a month, but knowing we had a date planned energized us to get through the hard parts of our weeks.

Emotional Roadblocks to Taking a Break

It may feel like getting out of the house together is simply impossible. We get it. We've been in that hopeless place and believed it would never happen. But we've come to realize there's never a good time to get away. If we waited until we knew for certain that both kids wouldn't have a medical crisis or that our daily life would be more stable, we would never leave.

It may never be easy for you to get away together. You still have to find a way if you want your marriage to thrive. We strongly encourage you to do everything you can to make it happen, and soon. Let's look at the different reasons it's difficult for you to plan a time away together. Put a check next to any of these challenges you face.

Challenges related to your child:

Anxiety about someone else caring for your child.

Worry about an emergency with your child.

Guilt about not spending that time helping your child.

Fear you won't be able to get back quickly enough if you need to.

Guilt for how leaving will be emotionally difficult for your child.

Embarrassment for feeling like a burden on family members or friends.

Worry about what other people will think about you leaving your child.

Challenges related to your marriage and future:

Concern that you won't be able to enjoy your time away.

Nervousness about spending time alone with your spouse or that you might have different expectations about sex.

Anxiety about leaving the house, stopping, and having time to think.

Fear that you may not want to come back.

Talk through Your Hesitancies

All your emotions are valid. At the same time, you may be able to work through your fears and take a break together. Try these four approaches to resolving your emotional roadblocks.

1. *Look at your concerns from a different perspective.* We used to be worried about what people thought about us leaving the kids so we could get away together. Then we considered the benefits for our children, including coming home stronger as a couple and less stressed as parents. We also realized that other people did not fully understand our circumstances.

2. *Process your emotions.* Many disability parents fear that if they leave, they might not want to come home. We have experienced this ourselves. Whatever is causing these emotions is impacting you, your marriage, and your family whether you leave the house or not. Talk through your thoughts and possible steps you can take to address these emotions.

3. *Accept that you will not be able to fully control what happens at home while you are gone.* There comes a point that, in order to leave the house, you have to be willing to accept that you will not be there if there is an emergency. This leads to the fourth approach.

4. *Prepare as best you can.* Put as much in place as you can to prevent emergencies and have a specific plan for if a situation does arise. To address the fear of not being able to get back in time, you may want to simply spend a night away just five miles from home.

Practical Matters as You Consider a Respite Break

Another way of working through some of your emotional roadblocks is by addressing practical details. Try these suggestions and start the planning process early.

Finding Quality Childcare You Trust

It can be very challenging to find someone you trust who is also trained in your child's medical or developmental needs. In the resources section, we provide information for numerous organizations that can help you find free in-home respite care and programs. Also, don't be shy in asking around about who other people use. These are just a few ideas for whom you can ask:

other parents at therapies, your child's school, or Special Olympics

your child's special education teacher or aides

therapists

doctors

social media groups

support groups

You can also:

Check with your child's Medicaid case manager.

Apply for a small state respite care grant to pay for a nurse or caregiver of your choosing for a couple of breaks.

Use the national respite program locator.

Look for churches in the area that offer respite break
programs.

Review the lists of camps for children with disabilities.

Contact local college and university nursing and special education departments.

Think creatively. Consider other special needs parents with
whom you could possibly swap caregiving one night a month. In
this situation, you will not feel like a burden because you're returning the favor, and who else better knows how to care for your
child than a parent facing similar challenges? Above all, pray that
God will provide a way and bring people into your life who can
support you.

Making Room in Your Budget

Be creative and resourceful. Plan inexpensive dates like a picnic
at the park, lakeshore, or beach; go hiking; sit in a coffee shop; or
just go for a walk. The most important part of getting out of the
house is just being alone together. If there is a certain place you'd
like to go but it costs money, think of some ways to temporarily
make a little extra money like doing yard work for a neighbor.

Taking Care of Preparations

Making all the arrangements can feel overwhelming. But every
time we leave the house and relax, we conclude that spending the
time and energy to get everything ready was so worth it. Begin
planning early and keep your care notebook and any other necessary documents regularly updated so all you have to do is print
them off. Here are some possible steps you may need to take:

Order medications and medical supplies.

Print a list of doctors' phone numbers.

Print an info sheet of your child's medications, allergies, and medical and developmental conditions.

Describe specific steps to take if your child becomes ill.

Print a tip sheet for how to manage behaviors.

Leave a goodie bag for your child each day with new sensory items, a stuffed animal, or their favorite toy.

If possible, meet with the new caregiver to orient them to your child's care.

Make sure your child's favorite snacks and meals are available.

The more you can do ahead of time to make things go smoothly for the caregiver, the more likely they will come back in the future and the better your child's experience will be.

Needing to Cancel

Of course, there's always the fear you'll get your hopes up and spend all that time planning, and you won't be able to go. That might happen. But there's a chance you will get to go and will have a wonderful time. Plan a flexible trip that has up to a twenty-four-hour cancellation policy (hotel, plane tickets, activities, and so on). And if you do need to cancel after the twenty-four-hour period, sometimes if you send in a hospital note, the company will still give you a refund.

Even if you only need to make very simple arrangements, we still recommend making reservations, because then you will have concrete plans.

Setting Expectations

Discuss your hopes for how you will spend your time together and come to an agreement in these areas:

How much time will you sleep in and rest versus go do activities?

How often will you check in with the caregiver?

Are you hoping to engage in physical intimacy?

How much spending money will you take?

Make It Happen

If you want to grow a thriving marriage, then planning a time to get out of the house together must take priority. For one couple, just getting out of the house for two hours might be a monumental feat that takes months of planning. Other couples may already have the resources and support to get away for an entire weekend. To plan a successful time away, you have to know where you are on that scale before you can make realistic plans.

Even if your getaway is just for two hours, the goal is to work up to a regular event out of the house together at least once a month. Prioritize and guard this time. Then, after establishing a caregiver and building more support, you can work toward escaping out of town (or in town) for one or more nights together. Try going away to a hotel in town for just one night. Sometimes we stay just twenty minutes away for one night. Even though we are just in a hotel close by, it still feels like an escape and we forget where we are. Staying close to home may help lower your anxiety too. Whether you're five or five hundred miles away, a getaway is a getaway. It makes such an incredible difference!

When you do get out, let go mentally as much as possible and be mindful during your time together. You can always call to check in, but then go back to being fully present with one another. If anything goes wrong, the caregiver will call you. No news is good news. Try to relax and enjoy your time. Even when it seems impossible, and you don't feel like you have the energy or finances, keep working to find a way to make it happen.

Begin to talk about how you would like to spend your time together. Don't build too high of expectations for the trip. We believe that getting out of the house together overnight should not just be about sexual intimacy. It's about spending time renewing your relationship, feeling close, having fun, resting, and talking. If you engage in sexual intimacy, that's a bonus! But that's not necessarily the goal of getting away together. In the next chapter, we will explore the barriers to engaging in sexual intimacy in caregiving marriages and how to cultivate that area of your marriage. For now, just plan a specific getaway for the two of you.

Build the Skills

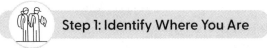 **Step 1: Identify Where You Are**

1. For the past month, how many times did you spend time together alone at home, and how long did it last?

_____

2. For the past four months, how many times did you spend time together outside the home, and how long did it last?

_____

3. How did you feel after those times alone together?

Wife:

_____

_____

Husband:

_____

_____

4. List any emotional or practical barriers to getting out of the house together.

_____

_____

_____

_____

Step 2: Set Your Goal

Create a respite break plan that takes your time alone together to the next level. (For example, if you've been getting out of the house together for a date night, consider setting the goal of getting one night away together in town. If you've been getting two hours alone together at home, consider working toward getting two hours alone together out of the house.)

1. Describe the break you'd like to take.

Where would you like to go?

_____

How long will you go? _____

What would you like to do?

_____

How would you like to spend your time together?

_____

2. List possible solutions for how you might overcome the barriers you've identified.

_____

_____

_____

_____

3. Set a specific date and time: _____

4. Choose a location: _____

5. Set your budget: $_____

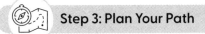 **Step 3: Plan Your Path**

List the concrete steps needed to make your break happen and put your name next to the steps that you will champion:

1. Secure caregiving:

_____

_____

_____

2. Make reservations:

_____

_____

_____

3. Make preparations:

_____

_____

_____

_____

4. Other needed steps:

_____

_____

_____

Set a deadline to finalize your plans: _____

Go do it! Try to relax. You've worked really hard to get away together. If you have to cancel, reschedule quickly.

Pray Together

God, we desperately need time for rest and recovery. The pace of our lives is sometimes overwhelming, and we miss the blessings you have placed around us. Thank you for your gift of rest. Provide a way for us to slow down our lives and take breaks together. There are so many worries we have about leaving our child(ren) with someone else so we can get away. Give us your peace and help us to trust in the care and support you place around us. Let us laugh, love, and play and come back energized and full of life! In Jesus's name, amen.

9

Enjoy One Another
on the Journey

Nurturing Sexual Intimacy

My beloved speaks and says to me: "Arise, my love, my beautiful one, and come away."

Song of Solomon 2:10 ESV

Todd: "It's been months since we've been intimate."

Kristin: "It's different for me. The nurse is right out there on the other side of the wall. And when she's not, the monitor's turned on. And I can't mentally turn off the stress in the house. We've got to get away together for a night."

Todd: "We can't get away every week. We can't even get out every month. You're just going to have to find a way to make it work at home."

As Todd became more frustrated and hurt and less understanding or emotionally supportive, Kristin became more and more uninterested and physically distant. The negative cycle grew stronger. We argued a lot.

Eventually, we learned the skills we want to share with you in this chapter: to listen to one another, try to understand our differences and disconnection, validate one another, and find a way to develop healthy sexual intimacy within our marriage.

We're not sex therapists, so we're going to leave advice about the physical mechanics to the experts. (We recommend some books in the resources section about how to make sex mutually enjoyable.) What we do know well is how it might feel like it's impossible to find a way to enjoy intimacy as caregiving parents. We want to focus on the importance of healthy sexual intimacy in your marriage, the unique barriers you may face, and how you can enjoy your sex life even as disability parents.

Nurture Your Relationship

It can be easy for a caregiving couple to pour all their time and energy into their child's needs at the expense of romance and intimacy. It might be tempting to just come to accept this is how it's going to be—that physical intimacy will be rare or nonexistent.

Your child's condition may be long-term, which means if you wait until your stress levels are lower or your circumstances improve, you may never have sex again. Yet, to grow a stronger marriage, physical intimacy should be a part of your relationship. Instead of letting your child's needs drive the two of you apart, determine that you will grow even closer through finding a way through this challenge together. We realize that, in certain situations, having sex just may not be possible right now due to a health condition, pain with sex, other sexual dysfunctions, or trauma. If you haven't already, be open with your spouse if you're dealing with any of these issues. Then look into finding a medical provider, pelvic floor specialist, or trauma therapist who can help you navigate these difficulties together. We encourage you, if at all possible, to begin to work toward reintegrating sexual intimacy into your relationship.

When you're physically separated, your child is in the hospital, you're working different shifts, or your caregiving demands increase, you may go through a season of agreeing that sex has to wait temporarily. But we encourage you to stay in communication during these periods and prioritize eventually finding time to draw closer together and enjoy one another, maybe in ways you never have before. Still talk about how you look forward to the next time you are able to enjoy sexual intimacy.

Levels of parenting demands and stress, positive and negative interactions with one another throughout the day, and sexual intimacy all influence one another. Factors that contribute to being able to maintain strong intimacy include keeping open communication, feeling emotionally safe and supported, sharing similar ideas about your marriage goals, making decisions together, sharing the caregiving role, relying on support networks, and depending on your faith in God.[1] Touching nonsexually, destressing together, giving affection, and helping one another with responsibilities will also increase sexual intimacy because they build your sense of connection. When spouses feel closer to one another, they often have an improved mood and handle stress better.[2] So, make it a priority to intentionally draw closer by spending time listening to each other's emotions and thoughts, holding hands, and kissing. Emotional and physical intimacy don't just happen. You will have to foster closeness while the stress attempts to pull you apart.

Prioritize Cultivating Sexual Intimacy

God has given married couples the special gift of sexual intimacy so you can express love, become one, and experience pleasure together in a way that isn't possible by any other means. God designed both men and women to enjoy sex and to seek pleasure in it.[3]

Based on his extensive research with married couples, John M. Gottman found that couples who have satisfying sex lives make it a priority. He puts it this way:

> Those whose sex lives were good to great made sex a priority rather than considering it the last obligation on a long to-do list. These couples talked about their sex life, ensured they had one-on-one time together, and put the relationship first, despite the competing demands of work and children.[4]

Gottman's statement takes on an even stronger meaning in the context of special needs parenting. There are numerous benefits of engaging in sexual intimacy together. Having sex can help you:

Draw closer emotionally, mentally, and spiritually.

Express love and feelings when it's difficult to use words.

Have fun together, laugh, and smile.

Relieve stress and tension.

Boost your mood.

Soothe one another.

Improve your physical and mental health.

Share mutual enjoyment.

We believe that engaging in sexual intimacy is one of the most important ways of coping as a couple while parenting children with disabilities. When you engage in physical intimacy, endorphins and hormones release that enhance your bonding and lower your stress.[5] It's also a unique way to escape together. It can be very difficult to let everything else on your mind go, but when you mindfully make love, you forget about everything else. You lose yourselves to one another. In her book *The Great Sex Rescue*, Sheila Wray Gregoire puts it this way: "Sex was designed to allow us to enter into a state of joyful abandon, to completely surrender ourselves to the other in an ecstasy of trust and love."[6]

Perhaps God has given caregiving couples the gift of sexual intimacy as a key way to strengthen their marriages while parenting their children with disabilities. We encourage you to keep an open dialogue, sharing your feelings and working together to make this special time possible.

Barriers to Sexual Intimacy

Disability parents often have a much more difficult time engaging in sexual intimacy than parents of children without disabilities.[7] There are so many challenging factors that can make it difficult to get uninterrupted, relaxing time alone together at home. Here are a few:

> your child's limited sleeping patterns or sleeping in the same room
>
> twenty-four-hour caregiving
>
> beeping medical machines
>
> your other children
>
> nurses, family members, or other people helping in your home

There are also some personal barriers to sexual intimacy:

> You believe you should be spending all your time taking care of your child.
>
> You feel guilty about enjoying yourself when your child is suffering or struggling.
>
> You have difficulty mentally separating from the stress in the house.

Your sexual intimacy may be the area of your relationship most impacted by the added stressors and responsibilities of caring for your child with disabilities.[8] Higher levels of mental, emotional, and physical stress can lower your sexual desire, decrease sexual satisfaction, and prevent you from spending time in activities that foster your emotional and sexual intimacy.[9] Similarly, high levels of stress, as well as conflict, depression, or anxiety, can drain emotional energy, which can result in less interest in engaging in sex, especially in mothers.[10]

Chronic stress keeps your body's stress response system activated, which can greatly decrease your sexual arousal and enjoyment.[11] In their book *Married with Special-Needs Children*, Marshak and Prezant explain how, especially for caregiving moms, stress can greatly lower parents' libido.[12] In fact, stress reduces both sexual interest and pleasure in 80–90 percent of both men and women![13] It might feel like it's just one more thing you need to do for which you don't have the emotional or physical energy left. And just thinking about having sex with your spouse may stress you out even more. We definitely don't want that to happen.

If you're chronically stressed, simply relaxing for a bit likely will not lower your stress levels enough to increase your desire for sex. You have to resolve your body's stress responses and calm your central nervous system.[14] In other words, you have to intentionally do something to address your stress levels, so you feel safe and secure. The stressful circumstances that are causing your nervous system to stay activated may never disappear, but there are ways to help lower your body's stress responses. The stress reduction strategies in chapter 4 can greatly help calm your body and mind, especially practicing mindfulness and the progressive muscle relaxation exercises. In addition, schedule planned breaks for each other. When partners get breaks to themselves, they have more emotional and physical energy and interest in sexual intimacy.[15]

Allowing yourselves to feel your emotions and have a good cry or engaging in nonsexual physical activity can also provide relief.[16] Sharing closeness and affection will tell your mind and body that you're okay. Soothing one another will help you feel calm and secure. The goal is to return to the state of feeling safe and not threatened. Discover what works to make your relationship a safe haven for one another.[17]

Address Serious Issues

Beyond these barriers, there may also be some more serious issues that you'll need to resolve before you're able to improve your sexual intimacy.

Identify Unhealthy Patterns

In a caregiving marriage in which one or both of you feel like you have little control over your circumstances, sex can become a way that you feel like you have a sense of control. You might be withholding sex from your spouse because creating boundaries around your body is a way that you can feel some control over your life, or you might be punishing them for something. Alternately, you might be initiating or pushing for *more* sex as an outlet to have control.[18] You might not even be aware that you are trying to achieve a sense of control in these ways, or you may feel like your spouse is attempting to control you through sex.

God intends for the "power" to be shared equally between spouses, so we shouldn't approach sex as an opportunity for control. Rather it's a space for mutual connection and celebration. Consider this passage in the Bible:

> The marriage bed must be a place of mutuality—the husband seeking to satisfy his wife, the wife seeking to satisfy her husband. Marriage is not a place to "stand up for your rights." Marriage is a decision to serve the other, whether in bed or out. (1 Cor. 7:3–4 MSG)

If you feel like either or both of you are approaching sexual intimacy in an unhealthy, nonmutual way, we encourage you to share your concerns with one another and go for marriage counseling.

Heal from Infidelity

An extramarital affair can cause serious and lasting harmful effects to your relationship, including creating a barrier to sexual intimacy. Working through the hurt and mistrust will take time, and you shouldn't feel pressure to rush back into engaging in sexual intimacy. Seeing a marriage counselor will likely benefit your relationship in this process.

Recover from Pornography Use

With the lack of time together, intense stress, potential emotional and physical distance, and need to mentally escape, one or both of you may have turned to pornography as an outlet. In *The Great Sex Rescue*, Gregoire shares insights from her extensive research on Christian married couples. She found that pornography use can greatly impact a couple's marriage relationship and sex life, typically by lowering the husband's sexual interest and performance.[19] Gottman explains that regular pornography use by a spouse can lessen the frequency of sex and communication during sex and result in less mutually satisfying sex. Porn can also increase the risk of betrayal through an extramarital affair.[20]

Pornography use by either spouse may become an addiction and will cause hurt and distrust. Remember, the spouse who is not engaging in pornography is not to blame. Spouses are not the cause of one another's sexual temptations, sins, or addictions.[21] If either of you has struggled with porn, we recommend you confess your behavior to your spouse and seek marriage counseling to work through this issue together.

Transition into Intimacy

Let's move on to the really good news! There are many ways you can journey toward increasing your desire for and enjoyment of sexual intimacy. That's where those other highly recommended books in the resources section come in. Go check them out together. Just keep in mind: if you've not been having sex, it can be more difficult for caregiving moms than dads to make the transition back to engaging in sexual intimacy.[22] Know that you and your partner likely have different levels of libido, and that 70.9 percent of women are not aroused before beginning to engage in sexual intimacy.[23] It literally does take getting in the mood, even more so for special needs moms.

Remember, to increase interest and desire for sex, you must first be nurturing your emotional intimacy and communicating in more meaningful ways. Drs. Les and Leslie Parrot describe it this way: "as you build a better talk life, your sex life will improve exponentially."[24] Also add in little moments of affection. In *The Gift of Sex*, Clifford and Joyce Penner recommend kissing passionately for at least thirty seconds every day.[25] You can also increase your sex drive by:

Exercising. Physical activity lowers stress and increases libido.[26]

Engaging in activities that help you destress, such as taking a hot bubble bath or shower.

Caring for your physical and mental health.

Seeing a doctor or mental health professional. Your lowered libido may be due to a physical health condition, depression, anxiety, a medication, pain with sex, other sexual dysfunctions, or a history of sexual abuse or trauma.

Take the pressure off one another. You both have to feel safe talking about intimacy. Think about sex in a new way: your primary goal is simply being close—uniting emotionally, spiritually, and mentally, not just physically. Clifford and Joyce Penner describe sexual intimacy this way:

> Lovemaking cannot be just physical . . . if there is to be a fulfilled relationship, there must be more to it than meeting physical needs. The total person—intellect, emotions, body, spirit, and will—becomes involved in the process of giving ourselves to each other.[27]

Engaging the total person will help you focus on all the positive aspects of spending intimate time together rather than just on a physical outcome (i.e., climax). Aim to simply grow closer and have fun. Openly talk about each other's wishes and needs. Compromise about frequency, take it slowly, and have patience.

And finally, to increase your times of sexual intimacy, you will need to be flexible and creative. In addition to getting outside the house together for respite care, find ways to begin to incorporate sexual intimacy back in at home. For example, consider taking a half day off work to stay home together while the kids are at school. If you're worried about a nurse or caregiver hearing you, go into your bedroom closet or another extra private space. Be open to taking advantage of any opportunity that presents itself, as long as the two of you are on the same page. There probably will be no perfect time to get away together or have sex, and the conditions likely will never be ideal, especially at home. But we've discovered that you just have to decide it's vital and find a way.

Build the Skills

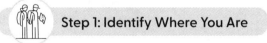 **Step 1: Identify Where You Are**

1. Intimacy is the combination of many factors. Rank these factors in your own marriage on the following scale:

(Disagree)	1	2	3	4	5	(Strongly agree)

We have open and honest communication.

Wife:	1	2	3	4	5
Husband:	1	2	3	4	5

I feel emotional safety and support.

Wife:	1	2	3	4	5
Husband:	1	2	3	4	5

We are good at making decisions together.

Wife:	1	2	3	4	5
Husband:	1	2	3	4	5

We share the caregiving role in a fair way.

Wife:	1	2	3	4	5
Husband:	1	2	3	4	5

We have a dependence on and faith in God.

Wife:	1	2	3	4	5
Husband:	1	2	3	4	5

We often engage in nonsexual affectionate touch (holding hands, kissing, hugging).

Wife:	1	2	3	4	5
Husband:	1	2	3	4	5

We spend regular time destressing together.

Wife:	1	2	3	4	5
Husband:	1	2	3	4	5

Sex is important to me.

Wife:	1	2	3	4	5
Husband:	1	2	3	4	5

Our sex life is enjoyable and satisfying to me.

Wife:	1	2	3	4	5
Husband:	1	2	3	4	5

Discuss any answers that might be surprising.

2. Identify barriers to sexual intimacy.

What personal barriers do you have?

Wife:

_____

_____

Husband:

_____

_____

What situational barriers to do you have as a couple?

_____

_____

3. Identify any specific serious issues to sexual intimacy.

We mentioned using sex to feel control, infidelity, and pornography as some examples. List any of those that apply:

_____

Other serious issues:

_____

_____

Step 2: Set Your Goal

1. If you came up with some more serious issues in your relationship, make a goal to work on those either with each other or through outside counseling. It is vital for you to begin to address those immediately, or they will tear your relationship apart.

Goal for addressing the issue(s):

_____

_____

2. **Choose one** of the following goals. Once you finish one, you can come back and try the other later.

Goal option 1: Pick a book from the resources section to explore more together.

Chosen resource:

_____

Goal option 2: Pick one of the factors that leads to greater sexual intimacy from step 1 and decide to work on it. (Make sure to come back to this exercise in the coming weeks and pick other factors after successfully improving one area.)

Wife's factor:

_____

Why did you choose it?

_____

Husband's factor:

_____

Why did you choose it?

_____

 Step 3: Plan Your Path

1. If you are working on a serious issue in your relationship, decide on a specific plan of action to address it.

Plan of action:

_____

_____

2. If you chose goal option 1:

a. Decide on how to get access to the resource—audio, hard copy, or other—and who will get it.

_____

b. Determine how you want to explore that resource, such as by reading a chapter or two and discussing it at night, skimming it for things that catch your attention, getting a night away and reading a little of it, and so on.

c. Write out your plan:

_____

_____

d. Set a date and time to do it:

_____

3. If you chose goal option 2:

Make a plan for ways each of you will specifically strengthen that factor in your marriage.

a. Plan of action for factor 1.

Wife:

_____

_____

Husband:

_____

_____

b. Plan of action for factor 2.

Wife:

_____

_____

Husband:

_____

_____

Bonus Goal

If you are in agreement about increasing your sexual intimacy, make a plan. It may feel awkward to plan it, but as disability parents, you are not likely to just have random opportunities.

When: _____   Where: _____

How can you reduce some of the barriers you identified to make the experience better?

_____

_____

Don't give up if your plan doesn't work out this time. Just keep trying to make opportunities for it to happen.

Pray Together

God, thank you for the gift of physical intimacy in our marriage. We know that closeness can feel complicated at times and that it can be a source of incredible connection and love, or it can be a source of pain and hurt. Lead us to find ways to make it a deeper part of our relationship, as you intend for us to experience joy and connection. Help us to heal from any hurts we feel from this area of our lives. Remind us daily of the many ways we can build intimacy without sex, and help us to grow a richer, fuller love with one another. In Jesus's name, amen.

10

Find Others to Travel Beside

Building a Strong Social Support Network

> For where two or three gather in my name, there am I
> with them.
>
> Matthew 18:20

The sinking sun has begun hiding behind the trees. You are in the woods attempting to build a shelter with only a rope and a tarp. Neither of you has any knowledge or experience beyond putting up a tent, so you're fumbling with the task. You argue over the best way to construct your shelter, but nothing is working. You're shivering, tired, and discouraged. At some point, you just give up and go with what you've created. The night is miserable. A cold rain blows in on you, and you end up sleeping on wet ground.

The next morning, you hear talking and laughing. You look at one another and jump up to go see who it is. Just a short way down the trail, you see another couple snuggling by their campfire.

"Hi there!" The woman smiles at you. "Come sit down and warm up."

You feel accepted as they listen to you describe your difficult evening. You see the understanding and compassion in their eyes. They look at one another, put out their fire, start packing up, and say, "Let's head over to your site."

Their reaction surprises you. "You don't have to do that!"

"Of course; we want to. We're going to come help the two of you."

It turns out this couple has also been through a very rough time, and they are now survival experts. They teach you how to build a shelter, show you how to collect the right wood and kindling to build a fire, and even cook you a hot meal. They listen to you and affirm that your journey *is* really difficult. They share some of their own story. You realize that though their experience isn't exactly the same as yours, you understand one another. Just being in their company is comforting.

There are other couples out there in the disability parenting wilderness. It may take searching for them, but they're out there— and they're probably going to be just as excited to see you as you are to find them.

Step Out of Isolation

If we could have a do-over, we would have found a caregiving parents' support group in our early years. Because we didn't, we felt like we were in a different world from everyone else and that no one in our small town was going through what we were. But we believed we didn't have the time or energy to go to a group and couldn't possibly find a way to build friendships with other parents. We didn't realize that such support would be critical for our marriage. We simply did not make it a priority.

But *there were* other parents going through similar experiences. Instead of reaching out, we isolated ourselves, which only worsened the strain between us. We missed out on emotional support and understanding, friendships, a safe place to process our grief and struggles together, and guidance for how to strengthen our marriage. We didn't have outside perspectives, advice from more seasoned parents, lifelines to resources, or help with problem-solving.

We aren't meant to travel this journey alone. But the reality is, for numerous reasons, caring for our children with chronic illnesses or disabilities can naturally isolate us. Disability parents commonly experience social stress, stigma, and embarrassment.[1] Have you ever felt alone on this journey, like no one else understands? Well, you're *not* alone.

You may feel like you've lost the support of some of your family members or friends since your child's needs became evident. It can be difficult for others to understand your child's disabilities or know how to support you. Also, the constant demands of caregiving make it difficult to hang out with other couples and families. By the time you plan for how to accommodate your child's needs and pack up all the gear, you're exhausted. Then you may end up having to leave early due to your child's sensory overload, behaviors, medical needs, or how people have treated you.

There are so many obstacles to spending time with others. However, social isolation creates serious problems for caregiving parents, including an increase in mental health symptoms, marital strain, and difficulty adapting. Lack of both formal social support and informal support from family and friends will cause increased stress on your marriage relationship.[2] On the flip side, couples who do engage in social connection and support foster resilience; lower their levels of stress, anxiety, and depression; and improve their mood. Support helps parents cope, adapt more quickly, and find positive ways of viewing their situations.[3] Support will help you maintain unity and stability in your marriage by buffering the effects of the stress and allowing you to invest in your marriage.[4]

Build Your Support Network

On this journey together, you will face difficulties you don't know how to handle. That's why it's critical to find others—some who are at a similar point on the journey, some who are much farther along the trail, and some who are on the path behind you. Caregiving parents need one another. If you've been able to stay close to your pre-diagnosis friends, that's wonderful. Many caregiving couples don't have the backing of family and friends. If that's true for you, it's even more important you reach out for support from other disability parents. Developing relationships with other parents of children with disabilities will foster connections that can provide deeper understanding and emotional support. You may even be able to find an older caregiving couple who can mentor you.

If you're struggling to find others in a similar situation, keep looking and praying for God to provide connection with others. You might find good friends at places in your normal routine. Strike up conversations with other parents at therapy appointments, Special Olympics practices, or school events. In the meantime, if you haven't already, join the organization for your child's disorder if there is one.

In addition, attending a formal support group together can strengthen your marriage by giving you a chance to talk about your struggles and be validated, grieve together, and receive help from other couples who have been there. Many churches, typically larger ones, offer support groups for caregiving parents as part of their disability ministries. You may not be very religious, or the group may be at a church or denomination you would not usually attend, but it still might be worth trying out. Children's hospitals, pediatric rehab therapy centers, and counseling centers also sometimes offer groups.

One of the biggest hurdles to attending a group together may be finding someone to care for your child while you're out. Many churches offer this service on location as part of the support group. If your child is homebound, prioritize finding in-home respite care during the support group hours. If attending a group together in person is just not possible due to your location or your child's needs, take turns attending the group and share with one another when you come home. There are even some live online groups for couples. Though in-person meetings are ideal, virtual support group meetings can be equally effective in helping lower disability parents' stress levels.[5]

Benefits of Attending a Support Group Together

Let's walk through some of the benefits of attending a support group together.

Feeling Understood and Encouraged

A formal group can be a safe place to speak openly. The act of just talking about your stress and grief can help you process and adapt and provide a healthy emotional release valve.[6] You can share about your feelings and struggles in your marriage and not receive judgment. Other couples can empathize with your situation because they know the ways that caring for a child with a disability can strain a marriage. You will likely hear that if other couples aren't currently having problems, they have in the past. Listening to other couples tell you your experience is normal can reduce your feelings of guilt and shame and open the door for more open communication with your spouse. A support group can provide comfort, encouragement, and a nurturing space where you can heal and strengthen your marriage.

Receiving Grief Support

Sharing your feelings of loss in a support group setting can be key in moving forward in your grieving process. Just as spouses can be in different places in their grief processes, different couples in the group will be at various points in their own processes. In this way, the same support group can help each couple at different points on their grief journeys. You will also likely reach higher levels of acceptance, adaptation, and adjustment by participating in a group.[7] Other couples can console you as they express empathy, share how they manage their grief, and help you move along in the process together.

Discovering New Hope and Perspective

When you first visit a group, make sure the atmosphere is caring and constructive and the group is led by an experienced facilitator. You want to leave feeling uplifted and supported and to sense you are growing as a couple. In addition to helping you process painful emotions, a formal group should also help you experience positive emotions such as hope. Listening to how other couples are persevering will challenge you to find new strength as a couple. Hearing other families' stories may inspire you to look at your life from a new perspective and see benefits and blessings in your situation. Other group members can also see your circumstances in a fresh way and make helpful suggestions for how you can grow closer and move forward together.

Processing Faith Questions and Struggles

Other group members have likely gone through similar spiritual difficulties or still are. You can travel this journey together. You can also learn how couples who are further along have resolved their faith crises and grown spiritually. They can help you process your own faith questions and heal spiritually. You can feel safe to share your shame-inducing thoughts and emotions about God, your marriage, and your child, and know that the other members have had similar thoughts. The two of you may be in different places in your faith. The leader and the group can help you work through your faith as a couple. The group can study Scriptures with you, pray for you, and encourage you. To heal and grow in your faith as a couple, you need this safe haven.

Learning Tips and Discovering Resources

The connections you make in support groups can help you save time and money searching for services for your child. Other caregiving parents can recommend free resources; suggest providers, therapists, and lawyers; give you tips; share about special activities; and help you solve problems. You can learn how other parents deal with challenges and receive their advice. This information exchange can be a vital part of your problem-solving processes as a couple. The more you know and understand about your child's needs, the more you'll be able to adjust and grow in accepting your child's disabilities.[8] The more you know, the more confident you will feel, which will lower anxiety and stress levels in your marriage.

Helping Other Couples

By attending a support group, you also have the opportunity to uplift others. Sometimes when we take the focus off our own problems to reassure others, we gain a new perspective on our situation. And encouraging other couples together will strengthen your bond with each other. You can share information with other parents, validate them, and pray for them. You can explain to other couples what's helped you strengthen your marriage or how you navigated a difficult season. Mustering the emotional energy may be difficult, but consider taking the time to support another couple. If you don't feel like you have anything to offer them, give them comfort by letting them know you're struggling too. Our compassionate God comforts us so that we can comfort others in their distress (2 Cor. 1:3–4). You just might experience joy in the process.

Building New Friendships

One of the most beneficial results of attending a local group is the opportunity to make friends. Hanging out with other couples and families will improve the health of your marriage and family. We realize that reaching out to other parents takes energy and vulnerability. But feel confident that you will be glad you did. You need at least one other couple who gets you and with whom you can fully share your heart. Nothing can replace the gift of having "couple friends" and being able to talk and pray wife-to-wife and husband-to-husband. We are blessed to have grown close to a couple who has two children with different disabilities. We feel like we can tell them anything, and they won't judge us. We know they will empathize and accept us. We have fun laughing together, and spending time with them renews our spirits.

Find a Church Home

If you haven't already joined a local congregation, we strongly encourage you to find a church home where you can grow in your faith together. Results from a large recent study by the Institute for Family Studies show that couples who regularly attend church together enjoy greater marital satisfaction and are less likely to divorce.[9] We understand it might be difficult to find a congregation where you can feel at home. When we moved back to the

In the resources, we provide two websites that offer a disability ministry church locator. You can also search for churches in your area that offer respite programs. Ask around where other disability families attend. Becoming involved in a vibrant faith community will give you a place to grow spiritually together, be prayed for, and pray for and serve others. You can fellowship with older couples and receive teaching, support, and resources to help you strengthen your marriage.

Nashville area, we visited thirteen churches before we finally found a congregation and worship service that worked with our family's complex needs. We experienced worship services that were too loud and overstimulating, children's programs that were too large and socially overwhelming, and buildings that were too difficult to access. We felt like we didn't fit in anywhere and would never find a church for our family. It was exhausting and disheartening, but we didn't give up.

A church probably doesn't exist that will fit your family's needs perfectly. You may not necessarily end up at a church with a disability ministry or even one with other families with disabilities. Sometimes small churches with fewer ministries can offer the loving extended family you need and will support you in ways a large church can't. If you're having difficulty finding a church, keep searching. Don't give up.

Regardless of the level of support you already have, you can always benefit from more social connection. The greater your support network, the more your stress levels will lower, and the more resilient your marriage relationship will be. Find courage together to take that next step toward building community.

Build the Skills

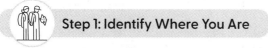 **Step 1: Identify Where You Are**

1. Step out of isolation.

In what ways are you socially isolated from family, friends, and other disability parents?

Wife:

Husband:

_____

What keeps you isolated? (Consider barriers due to your caregiving responsibilities, your child's disabilities, medical needs, challenging behaviors, your location, and your emotions and fears.)

Wife:

_____

Husband:

_____

2. Identify your current support.

What support do you currently receive in each of these areas?

Family:

_____

Friends:

_____

Other disability parents:

_____

A support group:

_____

Church home:

_____

In which areas do you need more support?

_____

_____

Step 2: Set Your Goal

Pick **one area** to strengthen within your support network.

Support area: _____

Step 3: Plan Your Path

List the steps for how you plan to strengthen that area of support:

_____

_____

_____

_____

Here's an example plan for locating a support group.

Step 1: Locate groups in your area. (Ideas for how to find a group: contact local children's hospitals, ask on social media, contact local disability organizations, ask at your child's therapy clinic, look for churches with disability ministries.)

Group 1: _____

Group 2: _____

Group 3: _____

Step 2: Contact the group leaders and take notes on what you learn.

Group 1:

_____

Group 2:

_____

Group 3:

_____

Step 3: Choose which group to try first based on the description and your schedule.

Step 4: Create a caregiving plan.

Step 5: Set a date to attend together: _____

Pray Together

God, we know you are with us. We also know you desire us to have others with us in life. Please bring us good friends with whom we can share life together, supporting one another. Please surround us with the support of people who love you. Thank you for the gift of connection with others. In Jesus's name, amen.

11

Have One Another's Backs

Parenting as a Team

Make every effort to keep yourselves united in the Spirit, binding yourselves together with peace.

Ephesians 4:3 NLT

Todd: "You let him get up from the table without eating his zucchini?"

Kristin: "You know that making him eat it won't end well."

Todd: "He needs to come back and sit there until he finishes it."

Kristin: "It's the texture. You know he gags. He can't help his sensory and feeding issues."

Todd: "I don't care. He needs to learn."

This was not our finest moment of parenting. Todd may have "won" that argument when our son was three years old, but it didn't feel like there were any winners that night as we cleaned up vomit.

You may be having difficulty knowing how to work together to care for all your child's needs, parent on their developmental level, or address their challenging behaviors. Regardless of your child's specific support needs, coparenting a child with any chronic illness or disability directly strains your marriage. This is why we are going to look at ways you can decrease your parenting stress and thereby improve the health of your marriage.

The good news is that a strong marriage helps cushion the negative impact of parenting stress. Your healthy relationship can help lessen symptoms of depression and anxiety you might experience as a result of parenting your child.[1] In other words, decreasing your parenting stress leads to a healthier marriage, and a healthier marriage decreases your parenting stress.

Consider the Parenting Stress on Your Marriage

When parents become stressed, their child's behavioral problems can increase, which can then increase parenting stress, anxiety, and depression, and on the cycle goes. Simply put, parents' and children's moods influence one another, which also directly affects the marriage relationship.[2] Tension, emotions, and behaviors can spill over from your interactions with your child to interactions with your spouse, and vice versa. So, days with more parenting challenges can cause more negative interactions between you and decrease positive exchanges such as kissing, hugging, or sharing a joke, even into the next day. Negative interactions with one another, such as disagreements about parenting, can also cause more stressful interactions with your child. Basically, your marriage relationship quality impacts how stressed you feel and how well you parent.[3]

The best way to reduce parenting stress is to expand your coparenting skills, which include:

Sharing the parenting and caregiving role.

Coming to agreement about your child's care needs.

Siding with one another and decreasing the frequency of parenting conflicts.

Increasing your level of support in responding to your child's challenging behaviors.

Decreasing your level of stress and remaining close by coparenting mindfully.

Practicing self-compassion and compassion toward each other.[4]

Share the Caregiving Role

When you worked together in chapter 3 to reorganize your daily responsibilities, you saw that you simply must split up and assign many of the tasks. But you both need to play a significant role in parenting and spending time with your child. With both of you involved, your child will have better developmental outcomes.[5] Watching one another care for your child will increase love and empathy for each other and will ultimately draw you closer together.

However, it's most likely not possible for the two of you to share the parenting role fifty-fifty. If one or both of you work outside the home, one of you will naturally play a bigger role in the daily caregiving. This is typical for disability parents. One parent is usually the primary caregiver and therapeutic support for their child with additional needs. This role division lessens time spent as a couple. Most often, the mother is the primary caregiver, but some fathers also assume this role.[6] Even though their interactions with their child play an important role in the child's development, fathers who work outside the home are often considerably less involved in the child's daily routine.[7] As a result, caregiving mothers often experience higher levels of psychological distress and more difficulty adjusting.[8] This is especially true if they don't feel supported by their spouse in caring for their children and managing difficult behaviors.[9] This can create distance and conflict and breed resentment.

Feeling unsupported in managing the parenting stress often leaves primary caregiving mothers emotionally drained and less likely to engage in sexual intimacy with their husband.[10] One study found that when fathers understood this frustration and took every opportunity to be more directly involved in their child's care, the mothers felt less stressed and more supported, and the couple experienced increased intimacy in their marriages.[11] Of course, the roles may be reversed in your marriage. Use the skills in chapter 5 to speak up and directly tell one another how you feel and ask for what you need. When both parents voluntarily share the caregiving role, couples have more positive interactions and higher levels of satisfaction.[12]

Agree about Evaluating Your Child's Needs

If your spouse has concerns about your child's health or development, listen carefully. Arguments can flare when one parent believes that their child needs services or interventions, but their spouse doesn't agree that it's a priority or needed. The spouse may oppose the intervention for several reasons, including financial cost, time constraints, or denial about the child's condition. They may even resent how much time their spouse is spending helping their child.

This period of seeking or receiving a diagnosis and securing interventions is often one of the most stressful times in the marriage.[13] Working together to look for information about the disorder and best approaches will unite you in your quest to help your child. Read about your child's symptoms or behaviors from professional sources such as the American Academy of Pediatrics, the National Institutes of Health, the Mayo Clinic, or children's research hospitals. One of you may feel a greater need to find more information. Share key research with one another about your child's disorder, treatment needs, and behaviors. Even if you don't understand as much as your spouse about advocating for your child at the doctor or school, if at all possible, go with your spouse to support them.

If you can't come to an agreement, get a professional evaluation from a medical provider or a child development specialist. This may mean getting on a wait list, but there's no harm in taking this step. You can always cancel the request later if you decide you don't need the appointment. If you meet with the provider and they have no concerns, then your loss may be time and a fee. However, the gains will be that the two of you agreed about going to the appointment, and now you have a professional assessment. It's imperative you work as a team to determine your child's needs and make decisions together to get your child the medical care and services they need.

Side with One Another

An intense conflict that caregiving parents often encounter is problematic family relationships. As a couple, you must decide how to deal with advice from your parents and other family members, or it can drive a wedge between you. For example, one set of grandparents might support your child's diagnosis and your efforts to get them needed interventions, while the other set of grandparents believe your child doesn't need special interventions. They may tell you that your child's difficulties are normal, and you just need to parent them correctly. To thrive as a couple, you must stand with one another as a team, regardless of what other family members or friends are advising you to do. Avoid taking a family member's side at the expense of supporting your spouse. Respond to family members in a united way. Later, you can discuss the issue privately.

Unite in Responding to Your Child's Behavior

Caring for a child with a disability or chronic illness can make coparenting significantly more difficult. Multiple factors can intensify your discussions about how to best parent your child, which can spark conflict. Traditional parenting and discipline methods likely won't be as effective or appropriate for your child with disabilities. You may not be able to base your responses on your child's age or developmental norms. Disagreements about the best approach for disciplining your child will challenge your marriage.

Deciding how to jointly respond to your child's behaviors can be complicated by medical conditions or any intellectual, developmental, or mental health disorders. Consider our zucchini argument at the beginning of the chapter. If a child is refusing to eat, it could be due to sensory aversions, noise, a feeding disorder, or stomach pain instead of—or in addition to—just not liking what's for dinner. Or, if a child is impulsive or emotionally reactive and has ADHD, ASD, sensory processing disorder, or any other developmental disorder, then punishment may be neither fair nor effective. If you're finding it difficult to understand your child's behavior or you can't get on the same page about how to respond to specific behaviors, seek a professional consultation and parent training. By soliciting professional advice, you can unite in your responses to your child's behavior, which will improve the health of your marriage and aid in your child's development.[14]

We decided to see a specialist to learn why Bethany Grace engaged in particular behaviors and how to respond to them well. With all of Bethany Grace's conditions, the therapist admitted that even she sometimes had difficulty determining the reasons for the behaviors and the best response. No wonder trying to parent together was causing conflict! And yet the specialist was still able to teach us how to praise Bethany Grace for appropriate behaviors and more effectively respond to problematic behaviors, which decreased their frequency. We also learned how to use visual supports and reward systems. As a result, Bethany Grace's development and happiness improved. She began to thrive. Learning from a professional helped us begin to consistently parent together, which greatly decreased our stress levels and arguments over Bethany Grace's challenging behaviors. We were able to share wins and see how it felt to combine our efforts to make a positive impact.

When you reach an impasse about how to manage your child's parenting needs or behaviors, seek additional advice from a professional. That way, it's an expert stating what will be most effective, not you telling one another. Have one another's backs, support each other's parenting, and be on the same page. Decide together on your child's most pressing parenting needs and focus on those. You can't address every issue at once. Consistency in parenting any child can be key, but especially when you're parenting a child with disabilities. Above all, remain focused on the goal of growing closer as a couple while parenting your child well.

Parent Mindfully

Kristin: While I stood at the stove with a spoon in each hand, stirring three pots, I tried to tune out the overstimulating noises of the kids playing. A high-pitched squeal pierced my ears, causing me to wince. Another squeal echoed in response. Our son charged through the house, eventually crashing into the kitchen cabinets. His younger sister followed and crashed into him. My eyes glazed over, and the sounds seemed to grow farther and farther away. I mindlessly continued cooking dinner as I parented on autopilot. I could predict what was about to happen. In the next thirty seconds, Bethany Grace pinched her brother, who then screamed and dropped to the floor. Then Bethany Grace began banging her head and crying. My pots began boiling over. I let out a loud groan of frustration as I stomped over to my children. I spent the next twenty minutes calming both kids. By the time they were calm, I felt even more exhausted and overwhelmed.

Kristin's above experience shows how stress levels can increase when we don't parent mindfully. We might think that mentally checking out helps us cope, but it ultimately leaves us even more drained and depleted. In chapter 4 we learned about how to practice living mindfully. Applying this concept to parenting your child will help improve your stress levels, emotional stability, marital relationship, and coparenting.[15]

Mindful parenting is being aware of our own thoughts, emotions, and body sensations; regulating our attention and emotions; being intentional; and taking a nonjudgmental and accepting attitude before reacting to our child.[16] Compared to the average couple, we may feel like we have less control over our parenting circumstances, which causes us even more anxiety. Mindful parenting can improve your mental health, support your grieving process, increase your levels of compassion for others and for yourself, enhance your family functioning, and create a more harmonious atmosphere.[17]

Being fully present with your child will increase your emotional connection with and acceptance of your child; reduce negative interactions; help improve your child's development; and reduce their problematic, aggressive, or self-injurious behaviors.[18] Parenting mindfully helps us become more flexible in our thinking, cope more adaptively, parent more calmly and with greater consistency, and find higher satisfaction in our parenting skills.[19]

Try these principles of mindful parenting:

Become fully present and aware of what's going on around you.

Recognize and accept your circumstances as they are in the present moment, whether pleasant or unpleasant.

Approach the situation with nonjudgmental acceptance of yourself, your child, and your spouse (this doesn't mean you necessarily approve of their behavior).

Listen to your child and spouse with full attention.

Observe emotions and nonverbal facial expressions.

Fully accept your child's unique needs and characteristics.

Become aware of your own emotions, thoughts, reactive impulses, and behaviors.

Set aside any unrealistic expectations.

Extend compassion to yourself, your child, and your spouse.

Respond with clarity and kindness.[20]

Invite God's Spirit into the Moment

As Christians, we can pray and ask the Holy Spirit to help us. While being mindful, we can become aware of God's presence inside us and all around us. As we breathe, the Spirit will fill us with love, joy, peace, patience, kindness, goodness, faithfulness, gentleness, and self-control (Gal. 5:22–23). We can focus on a verse of Scripture or whisper a short prayer like, "God, please give me your love and patience."

Become Mindful before Responding

Getting in the habit of pausing before reacting will also give you the opportunity to communicate with one another and make a unified parenting decision. When you remain fully present with your child and each other, you will be able to stop and discuss the situation. Then you can make a clear-headed joint decision as opposed to responding automatically out of emotions. Parenting mindfully will help you manage your stress reactivity.[21] When your stress levels are lower, you will respond more calmly out of self-regulation and control. Then, your child will also react less.

During stressful situations with your child, pause and practice a brief mindfulness exercise with your spouse like the ones we learned in chapter 4. Stop and take a deep breath together and remind one another to be mindful. Then you can together respond to your child. Over the years, the two of us have practiced this skill to the point that sometimes we only have to look at one another to confirm our united response. Coparenting mindfully will require you to be intentional and consistent, both as individual parents and in your interactions with your child as a couple.

When you parent mindfully, you can more effectively manage your child's challenging behaviors.[22] By fully participating, you can be more observant and curious about what's going on and think through all the factors. You can better understand yourself, each other, your child, and the situation. You can abandon

A brief exercise that can be very helpful is S.T.O.P.[23] When you feel yourself becoming overwhelmed or frustrated, use this one-minute, modified relaxation tool to reset before responding.

S: **Stop** whatever you're doing and step back.
T: **Take** three slow, deep breaths. Pay attention to your process of breathing.
O: **Observe** the present moment with your senses. Notice everything that's going on around you. What do you hear? See? Smell? Taste? What do you feel on or inside your body? What emotions do you notice? Simply notice everything you can, without judging anything as good or bad.
P: **Proceed** mindfully with a smile, engaging in what you need to do.

You can use this easy-to-remember tool anytime and anywhere to help you pause and be fully present before you respond. Also, practice this quick exercise two to three times throughout your day when things are calmer. The more you practice, the easier it will be to remember to be mindful in tense moments.

unrealistic views and expectations and respond more effectively, appropriately, and imaginatively to your child's developmental needs.[24]

If you're coming into a situation out of being half-present with your mind somewhere else, you are likely not going to know how to best respond and will automatically react. Thankfully, you can break out of this cycle and prevent escalation. Your child will feel truly listened to, validated, and better understood. Their problem behaviors will also likely decrease, which will, in turn, reduce the strain on your marriage. By modeling mindfulness and your resulting gentle responses, you can teach your child self-regulation skills. They may even begin to stop and take a deep breath themselves. When frustration begins to show on our faces, Bethany

Grace sometimes models to us taking a deep breath, because she's watched us do it so many times! ·

Kristin: In my kitchen, parenting mindfully could have looked something like this: As I stood at the stove stirring three pots, I felt the warm spoon in each hand and the steam rising as I listened and watched the kids loudly playing. I noticed that they both began experiencing sensory overstimulation and were becoming emotionally dysregulated. I became aware of the tension rising to my shoulders and anxiety filling my chest. I turned off the stove and took two deep breaths. As I slowly inhaled, I prayed, "Holy Spirit, fill me with your love." As I exhaled, I prayed, "I release my stress to you." I felt calmer. Then I walked into the family room. I gave our son a big bear hug to help soothe him, and then I held Bethany Grace in my lap, wrapping her in a blanket. I found them both separate quiet activities and got them settled before returning to the stove.

Practice Compassion toward Yourself

To experience less stress, you will need to lower your expectations. Everything can't be done perfectly, including your caring for your child. In fact, *everything* can't get done all the time. No one can do it all. When we set unrealistically high expectations and standards for ourselves, we are more susceptible to developing mental health disorders. Self-criticism and perfectionism are strongly linked to higher levels of depression and anxiety. In other words, when we harshly scrutinize ourselves as disability parents and spouses, seek approval from others, and worry about what other people think of us, we are setting ourselves up for poor mental health.[25] And we most certainly cannot hold ourselves to the same expectations society places on parents of children without special needs.

Instead of perfect parenting, a healthy goal is "good enough parenting." The idea of being a "good enough parent" has evolved from D. W. Winnicott's concept of the "good enough mother."[26] Good enough parenting is when we care for our child's emotional, physical, and psychological needs in a sensitive and responsive way.[27] However, this doesn't mean we are able to attend to 100 percent of their needs 100 percent of the time. It also doesn't mean we can parent perfectly or be able to do everything to improve their health and development. It's simply not possible. And it's not necessarily what our children need.

Let go of self-blame and guilt. Instead, set realistic expectations for your coparenting and for each other. Avoid holding each other to an impossible standard, and instead redefine what parenting success looks like for your family. Strive to simply do your best as a team. Todd's mom always used to say, "Do your best, and forget the rest." Saying this short phrase can reduce the pressure created by aiming for perfection. When you give up excessive self-criticism and practice self-compassion, you will respond less out of your own emotions, guilt, and self-doubt. You will be better able to meet your child's needs and comfort their distress.[28] Self-compassion and cognitive flexibility will also help you lower your levels of distress, improve your psychological well-being, become more compatible with one another, and better resolve conflict in stressful parenting situations.[29]

Believe you are going to be successful at good enough parenting and providing for all of your child's greatest needs.[30] You know you're amazing, loving parents, and you do everything you possibly can for your child. You've made decisions with your child's best interest in mind using the knowledge and resources you had at the time. You also love each other, and the two of you have been doing the best you can. So, give yourselves a break and decide to move forward without the weight of your self-criticism, guilt, or blame. Extend grace and compassion to yourselves both as individuals and as a couple.

And finally, be sure you have one another's backs. In all aspects of caring for your child, make sure you are supporting each other's parenting efforts. Your parenting stress will be one of the most turbulent forces that can weaken your marriage. Yet, if you work together as a team to love and care for your child, you can grow even closer and stronger through your parenting challenges.

Build the Skills

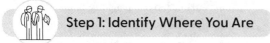 **Step 1: Identify Where You Are**

Reflect on how you currently share the caregiving role.

1. Describe your current delegation of the caregiving and parenting role. What percentage of the caregiving role do you fill?

Wife:

_____

Husband:

_____

2. How do you feel about the current arrangement? How would you like the way you care for your child and parent together to differ?

Wife:

_____

_____

Husband:

_____

_____

3. In what ways do you feel supported by your spouse in your caregiving? How can they support you better?

Wife:

_____

_____

Husband:

_____

_____

4. In what ways are you successfully parenting together?

Wife:

_____

_____

Husband:

_____

_____

Reflect on how you agree or disagree about your child's needs.

1. What concerns do you currently have about your child's health or development?

Wife:

_____

_____

Husband:

_____

_____

2. What areas of your child's health or developmental needs do you agree on?

Wife:

_____

_____

Husband:

_____

_____

3. In what areas concerning your child's care needs are you experiencing disagreement?

Wife:

_____

_____

Husband:

_____

_____

Reflect on how other people's opinions cause parenting conflict.

1. In what ways do others, including family members, influence your parenting decisions?

Wife:

_____

_____

Husband:

_____

_____

2. In what ways are these influences healthy? In what ways are these influences unhealthy?

Wife:

_____

_____

Husband:

_____

_____

Reflect on how you currently respond to your child's challenging behaviors.

1. How often do you agree about how to handle your child's problem behaviors?

Wife:

Never	Rarely	Sometimes	Often	Very often

Husband:

Never	Rarely	Sometimes	Often	Very often

2. For which behaviors do you agree on what an appropriate response should be?

Wife:

....

....

Husband:

....

....

3. For which behaviors do you disagree on what the appropriate response should be?

Wife:

....

....

Husband:

....

....

Reflect on ways you do and don't parent mindfully.

1. Rate your current levels of parenting stress.

Wife:

Very low stress	1	2	3	4	5	6	7	8	9	10	Very high stress

Husband:

Very low stress	1	2	3	4	5	6	7	8	9	10	Very high stress

2. How often do you judge your spouse or child?

Wife:

Never	Rarely	Sometimes	Often	Very often

Husband:

Never	Rarely	Sometimes	Often	Very often

3. How likely are you to pause before reacting or delivering a parenting decision?

Wife:

Not likely	Somewhat likely	Likely	Very likely

Husband:

Not likely	Somewhat likely	Likely	Very likely

4. How aware are you of your own emotions when interacting with your child?

Wife:

Not aware at all	Somewhat aware	Aware	Very aware

Husband:

Not aware at all	Somewhat aware	Aware	Very aware

5. What strategies have you found that help you manage your parenting stress and parent well?

Wife:

_____

_____

Husband:

_____

_____

Reflect on how you do or don't parent with self-compassion.

1. How often do you self-criticize, self-blame, or strive to be a perfect parent?

Wife:

Never	Rarely	Sometimes	Often	Very often

Husband:

Never	Rarely	Sometimes	Often	Very often

2. In what ways have you observed your spouse self-criticizing or self-blaming?

Wife:

_____

_____

Husband:

_____

_____

3. In what ways do you feel criticized or blamed by your spouse?

Wife:

_____

_____

Husband:

_____

_____

Step 2: Set Your Goal

Choose **only one** of the following six areas as a couple and set a goal to try this week. Then try the other areas in the following weeks.

1. Share the caregiving role.

Set one specific goal for how you are going to better support one another in caregiving and parenting:

_____

2. Agree about your child's needs.

Decide on one concern about your child you agree to work on together to determine their best care needs:

_____

3. Side with one another.

Set one goal for supporting each other's parenting as you integrate advice or influence from others:

_____

4. Unite in responding to your child's behavior.

Set one goal for uniting more in your responses to your child's challenging behaviors:

_____

5. Parent mindfully.

Determine one goal for parenting more mindfully together:

_____

6. Parent with self-compassion.

Choose one way you will help one another practice greater self-compassion:

_____

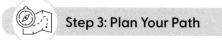 **Step 3: Plan Your Path**

Complete **only** the area you chose in step 2.

1. Share the caregiving role.

What one step will you take together to share the caregiving role more?

_____

2. Agree about your child's needs.

What one step will you take together to address the area of concern you have identified?

_____

3. Side with one another.

Decide on one way you will side together the next time you experience tension in interacting with family or friends regarding your parenting:

---

4. Unite in responding to your child's behavior.

Decide on one way you will jointly respond to your child's challenging behavior:

---

5. Parent mindfully.

Plan one way you will practice parenting mindfully together (e.g., practice S.T.O.P. together):

---

6. Parent with self-compassion.

Plan one way you will help each other practice greater self-compassion (e.g., when you hear your spouse self-blaming or self-criticizing, express compassion to them and remind them they are doing their best):

Pray Together

God, it can be so challenging sometimes to parent our child together. We admit that we don't even know how to sometimes, but we are doing the best we can. Heal us from any unwarranted guilt or shame from our choices and teach us through our mistakes. Help us to slow down and be present with our child and each other, so we can reflect the care, love, and value you have shown for each one of us. Allow us to work as a team both for the good of our child and also for the ways that it will build our marriage relationship. Bring us unity and strength in our decisions and grace in our responses. In Jesus's name, amen.

12

Call Out for Help

Seeking Professional Mental Health Treatment and Marriage Counseling

I waited patiently for the Lord to help me, and he turned to me and heard my cry. He lifted me out of the pit of despair, out of the mud and the mire. He set my feet on solid ground and steadied me as I walked along. He has given me a new song to sing, a hymn of praise to our God.

Psalm 40:1–3 NLT

content warning: suicide attempt

Kristin: The day after the traumatic cesarean section, I was already reliving the nightmare pregnancy and six minutes of fetal distress several times a day. Then, over the next several months, I watched Bethany Grace go into numerous medical emergencies. The flashbacks grew stronger, and my depression grew deeper to the point I couldn't function.

I couldn't hold on much longer. The nonstop caregiving, financial pressure, and marriage problems sent me spiraling into a dark pit. It was too much. I finally worked up the courage to tell Todd how bad my depression had become.

"I think I need to go to counseling. I feel really depressed, and I can barely function with my anxiety. I keep reliving the traumatic pregnancy and emergency delivery over and over," I said, and tried to hold back my emotions to keep the dam from bursting.

Todd responded with, "We don't have the money for that. And how are you going to leave the house? I have to work. You'll be okay."

But I was far from okay. I was at my breaking point. Was he afraid about what people at church would think if I went for professional help? I didn't know what to do. I was desperate to escape my distress.

Todd: I knew Kristin was having a hard time, but so was I. We had a job to do as parents, and we just had to suck it up and take care of our responsibilities. Because I compartmentalized things, I was able to function just enough to keep going, and I assumed she would do the same. Our kids couldn't survive life on their own, but she was an adult, and I expected her to be able to handle her own stuff. I was on the verge of breaking myself, and the extra weight of trying to help her was going to put me over the edge. Eventually I didn't even have the energy to ask how she was doing, because I knew I couldn't handle the answer. It seemed better to not even bring it up anymore and just keep focusing on what had to be done.

Kristin: By the time Todd realized the seriousness of my mental health crisis, it was too late. He finally supported me going for help when Bethany Grace was a year old. I faithfully attended therapy and took the different antidepressants the psychiatrist prescribed. But nothing helped. My therapist even confessed, "You're slipping through our hands. We don't know how to help you."

I stopped eating and stayed in bed all day. My parents had to come live with us to care for the kids and keep life going. I was done. I didn't want to live anymore. Everything was too overwhelming and painful.

Todd: When I walked into the room and saw Kristin on the bed, I was numb. I had seen her struggling, and I had tried to listen and help where I could. I truly had been supporting her the last few months, but I'd felt helpless in the whole process and like my efforts meant nothing to her. No matter how hard I tried or encouraged, it didn't seem to make a difference. I felt the only way she would make it out of her depression was to decide to do so herself. But, as I looked at the pills strewn on the bed and her motionless body, I realized she'd decided on another way out. I was heartbroken for her, sad for our children, and overwhelmed with questions about how I was going to be able to make it in a future without her. This was all in the span of half a second, as I pulled out my phone to call 911.

Kristin: I woke up in the intensive care unit four days later after having survived on a ventilator. The doctors couldn't explain how I'd lived. There was no medical explanation. God had given me a second chance. But I still had to learn how to desire to live with my same painful circumstances. If I had gone for professional help at the first signs of my trauma response, depression, and anxiety, my mental health likely wouldn't have deteriorated so severely. Now we both know there's always hope and, no matter the cost, we have to seek help.

Know Your Risk

Mental health issues are a significant concern for disability parents; we experience stress, anxiety, anger, and depression at significantly higher levels compared to the national average. In fact, we have two times the risk for developing clinical mental health symptoms.[1] It's been found that 31 percent of parents with children with intellectual and developmental disabilities (IDD) experience clinical depression and anxiety.[2] That's about one in three disability parents! This means a significant percentage of caregiving marriages will be strained by a spouse's mental health condition. Being aware of your risk and addressing concerns early will serve your mental health and help you care for and support one another.

While disability fathers develop depression at a higher rate than both mothers and fathers of typically developing children,[3] disability mothers experience depression and anxiety about their children's futures more than disability fathers.[4] Mothers of children with disabilities also have up to three times the risk for developing clinically significant levels of stress, anxiety, and depression compared to mothers of typically developing children.[5] This is for several reasons. In general, women in the United States develop depression at higher rates than men.[6] In addition, the Centers for Disease Control and Prevention (CDC) reports that about one in eight women who have recently given birth experience symptoms of postpartum depression.[7]

As we've mentioned, mothers are typically at home more, which means they manage the challenging behaviors or care for their children's medical conditions all day.[8] Not working outside the home may contribute to lower levels of life satisfaction and higher levels of anxiety and depression.[9] Traumatic experiences during the mother's pregnancy or medical events with their child can also significantly increase their risk for developing post-traumatic stress disorder (PTSD), depression, and anxiety. Numerous studies have shown that approximately 19–20 percent of parents of children with chronic physical illnesses and a history of medical treatments meet the criteria for PTSD.[10]

Mental health care will be a key factor in determining the health of your marriage and family. If one or both of you are depressed, it can lower the quality of your relationship and impact how you feel about the future of your marriage relationship.[11] If depressed, you may view your marriage through a lens of hopelessness. You also will likely not enjoy activities together and may have a lowered sex drive. Your moods impact each other's. Depression is contagious and can block communication, cause frustration, interfere with problem-solving, and impact parenting.[12] Chronic stress, in combination with depression, can lead to suicidal thoughts and actions. Mental health disorders also increase your risk for developing substance abuse and addiction.[13]

Recognize the Signs

It can be difficult to know if your reactions and feelings are typical responses for caregiving parents or if they are signs of a more serious mental health condition. With the waves of chronic grief and daily stress, how can you tell if you need professional help? The National Institute of Mental Health recommends seeking a professional mental health consultation if your mood has begun to negatively affect your level of daily functioning and persists for two weeks or longer,[14] or you resonate with any of the following symptoms. Reflect and see if any of these negative thoughts regularly fill your mind:

> *I feel so overwhelmed.*
> *Nothing is ever going to get better.*
> *I don't want to be around other people.*
> *It's hard to get motivated to get out of bed.*
> *Alcohol or pills help me cope.*
> *I'm so anxious I have a hard time functioning.*
> *I don't enjoy much anymore.*
> *I feel worthless.*

Determine if you've experienced any of these behavior patterns:

> Crying often.
> Reliving traumatic experiences over and over.
> Eating or sleeping more or less than usual.
> Having difficulty concentrating.

If any of these statements resonate with either of you, share your experiences with each other and consider these additional questions:

> Are your symptoms impacting the quality of your daily life and/or your family?

If you are in crisis or worried about your safety or the safety of someone else, chat at 988lifeline.org, text HELLO to 741741, call the Suicide & Crisis Lifeline at 988, or go to your nearest emergency department.

Have your symptoms lasted for two weeks or longer?

Are you concerned or have others expressed concern about your mental or emotional well-being?

Are you wishing you were dead or having thoughts about harming yourself? **If so, seek help immediately.**

One spouse might notice concerning changes in the other before they see it themselves. Express concern if your spouse:

Behaves out of character or acts impulsively.

Seems anxious, nervous, apathetic, or irritable.

Avoids talking to friends or family.

Cries or appears sad often.

Stops caring for their person—not showering or caring about their appearance.

Disappears for significant amounts of time with no explanation.

Becomes less active or interested in fulfilling responsibilities, including caregiving.

Increases their consumption of alcohol or uses drugs.

Makes hopeless statements.

Get directly involved in seeking immediate help if your spouse:

Talks about death or wanting to die.

Threatens to hurt themselves.

Puts their affairs in order.

Gives away their possessions.

Writes unusual apology or goodbye letters.

Purchases a firearm or stashes pills.

If your spouse is showing any of these serious signs, ensure that they immediately receive a mental health assessment at either a crisis walk-in center, an emergency department, or a psychiatric hospital. Don't leave them alone. Lock up any firearms, medications, ropes, and sharp objects.

Seek Help as Soon as Possible

If you think that you might be experiencing symptoms of depression, anxiety, PTSD, or another mental health disorder, please seek professional help as soon as possible. Go before you get to the point that you feel like nothing's working. The sooner you seek treatment, the better your outcome will be, especially when trauma is involved. Keep in mind that men's symptoms may look different from women's, and men typically seek treatment much less often. By the time they do seek help, their depressive symptoms may be more severe.[15]

You can follow these steps for finding a mental health provider:

1. Ask your friends for referrals.
2. Call your insurance company or look through your "covered providers" list online.
3. Use an online therapist locator.
4. Screen the list of providers by asking around, checking reviews, and reading their websites.
5. Eliminate therapists who are not trained to meet your specific treatment needs, especially trauma.
6. Schedule a phone consultation.

7. Meet with the therapist for an intake. Think of this time as if you are interviewing them for a job. Remember, this is your life and your care.

8. Schedule a second appointment if you believe they might be a good fit, they can help you, and you feel comfortable with them. If not, meet with another therapist.

9. Discuss with your therapist if they think you should meet with a psychiatric provider to find out if medication might help improve your symptoms.

10. In five to six weeks, reassess with your therapist if you feel like you're making progress. Speak up if you feel like you're not getting any better or you believe therapy isn't helping.

The potential benefits of going to therapy include:

Talking openly about your struggles.

Exploring your grief and emotions.

Gaining a new perspective about your marital issues.

Developing new coping skills.

Learning how to ask for what you need.

Experiencing improvement in your mental health symptoms.

Processing and recovering from trauma.

If you think therapy or medication might help you, then make it happen. Given your daily stress and grief, you almost certainly will experience value from going, even if you don't feel like you're at a breaking point. We believe that all disability parents can benefit from counseling. Ultimately, you have to decide to seek help for yourself, regardless of what anyone else thinks.

Kristin: I hadn't realized how trauma could impact my daily functioning and mental health or that there were treatments that could improve my symptoms and quality of life. Bethany Grace was five years old before

EMDR has been shown to be especially effective for caregiving parents who have experienced a traumatic event with their child. Symptoms of PTSD can include:

flashbacks or reliving the traumatic experience
nightmares about the experience
avoidance of memories, thoughts, feelings, or situational triggers of the event
psychological or physiological distress in response to reminders[16]

someone recommended Eye Movement Desensitization and Reprocessing (EMDR) therapy to me. The first EMDR therapist I met didn't seem like a good fit, so I asked around and found another therapist, and they were excellent. I'm so thankful I began the treatment. It has changed my life. I no longer relive the nightmare events. I still become a little upset sometimes when something triggers my memories, but my physical and emotional reactions are at a fraction of the intensity that they used to be.

Seeking trauma treatment as soon as you identify your symptoms will help prevent the worsening of your symptoms, and your recovery can be quicker.[17] If Kristin had gone for trauma treatment soon after Bethany Grace's birth, we're confident that her mental health wouldn't have declined the way it did. If you're struggling with symptoms of PTSD, make sure to research and find a trauma therapist who is expertly trained in EMDR.

Support Your Spouse's Care

Effectively supporting your spouse while not enabling their unhealthy behaviors requires patience, understanding, and balance. If you suspect that your spouse is experiencing a mental health condition, keep the following important tips in mind.

Help your spouse seek treatment:

Learn about mental health disorders.

Listen and ask questions.

Encourage them to seek professional help but avoid pushing too hard.

Make going to therapy a financial priority.

Help them find a provider and offer to go with them for the first appointment.

Provide childcare so they can go.

Encourage them to consider seeing a doctor about the possibility of trying a medication.

Support your spouse at home:

Stay positive.

Avoid blaming or shaming.

Ask how therapy sessions are going.

Encourage faith and prayer in addition to seeking professional help.

Avoid telling them to get over it or that it's possible to think their way out of it.

Do something fun together.

Encourage them to continue to fulfill their responsibilities throughout the day.

Support their self-care and physical activity.

Take care of yourself:

Don't take their lack of interest in you personally.

Maintain self-care of your mental and physical health.

Consider seeing a therapist yourself.

Join a support group for spouses, such as the National Alliance on Mental Illness (NAMI).

Marriage Counseling

We've met with a marriage counselor at different times throughout our twenty-two years of marriage. Each time, we knew we needed a professional to help us work through our impasses, stress, grief, and hurts. There are many situations where meeting with a licensed marriage counselor can greatly benefit couples. Ideally you could find a licensed Christian marriage counselor. A counselor can help if you feel like you're no longer in love, you're disconnected emotionally, you have trust issues, you're struggling to resolve conflicts, or you just can't relate to one another in healthy ways. Having a counselor's outside perspective can help the two of you see your situation in a new way or remind you of skills or resources you've overlooked.

Even if neither of you are struggling with mental health issues, all caregiving couples can benefit from speaking with a counselor. A good counselor will be unbiased and help you build on the strengths you already have in your marriage. Even if you feel like your marriage is doing well, your marriage will still grow stronger from having a safe and facilitated space to work through matters together. If the two of you are struggling through an issue on your own, now might be the time to reach out for additional professional support. Make sure to research providers and choose a counselor that specializes in couples' therapy. If possible, find someone experienced in working with families with disabilities.

Here are some situations in which we strongly advise you to seek professional marriage counseling right away:

verbal, emotional, or physical abuse from one spouse
symptoms of a mental health disorder or an addiction
extramarital emotional or sexual infidelity

difficulty enjoying sexual intimacy or a history of sexual abuse
unresolved trauma

Between 70–75 percent of motivated couples who attend marriage counseling remain symptom-free long-term. Yet most unhappy couples wait an average of six years before they go for therapy.[18] Counseling can strengthen your relationship by helping you learn to communicate better, resolve conflict, connect emotionally, heal together, improve intimacy, and work through any other concerns, such as stress and grief, that you may have. Counseling can also prevent problems from developing, which can be up to three times more effective than intervention.[19] In other words, don't wait. The sooner the better!

Explore Any Hesitations to Counseling and Treatment

If one or both of you are reluctant to start the process of seeking either marriage counseling or individual treatment, explore your hesitations to see if you are facing any of these barriers and consider the provided solution.

If you lack the motivation or emotional energy:
　　Ask your spouse, a family member, or a friend to encourage you and help you start the process.

If it's not in your budget:
　　Call your insurance company or contact therapists and agencies that offer a sliding fee scale based on income and extenuating circumstances. Some churches offer assistance with the cost of therapy too.

If one spouse isn't willing to go or support the other in going:
　　Keep gently raising the issue by expressing concerns and explaining the importance of mental health and the

health of your relationship. Say things like, "I want us to feel closer and be happier. I think that a counselor can help us get unstuck." If one spouse continues to resist marriage counseling, the other spouse may need to decide to go for treatment on their own for the sake of their own mental health.

If you have no one to care for your child:

This may be the toughest hurdle to overcome, but it's crucial you find a way. Utilize respite care organizations (see the resources section). Remember that your mental health and marriage relationship are the top priority if you want to care for your child well.

If you want to keep your business private and are afraid of what others will think:

Except in cases where one spouse may be in physical danger, no one outside your marriage needs to know you're seeking marriage counseling or individual treatment if you don't want them to. Ultimately, you are the ones who are going to remember and be impacted by your decision.

If you fear the therapist will judge you, side with one spouse, or tell you what to do:

The goal of a professional therapist will be to offer a neutral perspective and to guide you in the process of growth rather than telling you what to do. Therapists are some of the most compassionate and accepting people.

If you think therapy will be too hard:

Therapy is hard work. But so is marriage and so is your life. Therapy can improve your life and, in some ways, make it easier.

If you fear therapy will make things worse:

Remember, as we've seen, the research shows that if you're motivated, the odds are strong that individual and/or marriage therapy is going to help your marriage and mental health.

If you're afraid of being hospitalized:

Only in the most extreme cases do mental health professionals involuntarily commit a client. Hospitalization is typically a temporary last resort, and its main goal is to keep you safe through a crisis period.

If you feel like getting professional help means you're a failure:

Shame, or telling ourselves that there is something wrong with us, can keep us from going for treatment. Going to therapy or taking medication doesn't mean you're a failure or that there's something wrong with you or your marriage. On the contrary. Having the courage to go indicates you are strong and committed to investing in your marriage and health.

Overcome the Stigma

A prevailing stigma surrounding mental health disorders and seeking treatment still exists in our society. Due to efforts to raise awareness, more people and organizations are beginning to acknowledge that mental health conditions are biological medical disorders. But a strong fear of this stigma still prevents many people from seeking treatment. It's even more difficult for Christians to step out in courage to seek professional help. Christians, and especially more conservative Christians, are less likely to seek treatment than non-Christians. Their faith beliefs, the opinions in their churches, and fears of what others might think hold them back and lower their willingness to go for treatment.[20]

Many Christians believe depression, anxiety, and other mental health disorders are solely a personal spiritual issue. Christians have higher self-stigma of depression than non-Christians.[21] They blame themselves and may attribute their condition to problems in their relationship with God. Christians may believe their mental health symptoms are due to their sin, they just need to pray harder, and if God doesn't heal them it means their faith is weak. But due to not seeking treatment for their symptoms, they have poorer mental health outcomes.[22]

Continued mental health symptoms or addiction do not equal weakness or lack of faith. Mental health conditions are typically biological medical illnesses that often also require professional psychiatric and psychological treatments. Depression and anxiety, among other mental health disorders, are partly due to an imbalance in brain chemicals and altered neural circuits exacerbated by stress. In many cases, medication may improve symptoms. A combination of therapy and medication is typically most effective in improving symptoms.[23]

Address Both Faith and Mental Health Struggles

Faith and mental health struggles are often intertwined. As we learned earlier, disability parents are at greater risk for experiencing faith struggles in addition to mental health conditions.[24] Religious and spiritual troubles often contribute to mental and physical health problems, and vice versa.[25]

Many Christians first seek pastoral counseling for faith struggles and/or mental health concerns. We encourage you to meet with your pastor or a biblical counselor, especially if you are wrestling with spiritual questions or experiencing problems in your faith and relationship with God. However, if you're experiencing any mental health symptoms, we recommend you also seek professional mental health treatment in conjunction with pastoral counseling. You might consider finding a licensed Christian counselor who can help you work through both your spiritual and mental health struggles simultaneously.

Now, we're not saying by any means that God may not heal a person's mental health disorder or marriage through prayer and faith alone. Sometimes he may. But marital issues and mental health conditions don't typically improve through praying and waiting alone. Perhaps a sign of your strong faith would be stepping out in courage and trusting God to help you heal and recover through a therapist, a physician, a pastor, medication, speaking with others, and/or a caregiver support group. Your mental health recovery, marriage healing, and faith restoration will likely need a combination of spiritual counseling, professional treatment, Christian community, and prayer.

Our strength ultimately comes from relying on God for guidance, help, and joy. God is the center and presence in our recovery and healing processes. And so, there's always hope.

Build the Skills

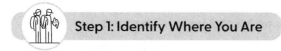 **Step 1: Identify Where You Are**

Recognize the signs.

1. Review the list of mental health symptoms listed in the "Recognize the Signs" section of this chapter. List any of the thoughts or symptoms that resonated with you personally and add any additional potential concerns that you have about your mental health.

Wife:

_____

_____

Husband:

_____

_____

2. List any of the signs you have noticed in your spouse and any additional concerns you may have.

Wife:

_____

_____

Husband:

_____

_____

3. If one or both of you are experiencing mental health symptoms, how has your marriage been impacted?

_____

Consider the benefits of seeking treatment.

1. In what ways might going for treatment help your mental health and your marriage?

_____

_____

2. Review the major indications and recommendations for marriage counseling. List any that apply to your marriage:

_____

_____

3. List any other reasons you think you might benefit from marriage counseling:

_____

_____

4. In what ways would counseling be beneficial for preventing problems in your marriage and strengthening your relationship?

_____

_____

Identify barriers to going for help.

1. List any obstacles or fears that might prevent you from going for treatment.

Wife:

_____

_____

Husband:

_____

_____

Reflect on faith struggles.

1. Describe any ways that you are struggling in your faith personally or as a couple and any ways you think your faith and mental health might be interconnected.

Wife:

_____

_____

Husband:

Step 2: Set Your Goal

Choose **only one** area for now and set a goal.

1. *Strengthen your mental health*. List one current goal you have about improving or strengthening your mental health.

Wife:

Husband:

---

2. *Seek individual help.* List one current goal you have about seeking individual mental health treatment.

Wife:

Husband:

---

3. *Support your spouse.* Name one goal you have for how you would like to support your spouse's mental health.

Wife:

_____

_____

Husband:

_____

_____

4. *Go for marriage counseling.* List a goal you share as a couple regarding attending marriage counseling.

_____

_____

5. *Overcome barriers and fears.* List a goal you have for overcoming your challenges to seeking help:

_____

_____

6. *Address faith struggles.* List any goals you have for strengthening your faith or for processing spiritual struggles or conflicts you are experiencing as a couple.

Wife:

_____

_____

Date you will take this step by:

_____

Husband:

_____

_____

Date you will take this step by:

_____

Step 3: Plan Your Path

Complete **only** the section for the one goal you chose for now.

1. *Strengthen your mental health*. What first step do you plan to take toward strengthening your mental health?

Wife:

_____

Date you will take this step by:

_____

Husband:

_____

Date you will take this step by:

_____

2. *Seek individual help.* What first step do you plan to take toward finding a provider?

Wife:

_____

Date you will take this step by:

_____

Husband:

_____

Date you will take this step by:

_____

3. *Support your spouse.* What one step will you take in the next two weeks to support your spouse's mental health?

Wife:

_____

Husband:

_____

4. *Go for marriage counseling.* What one step do you plan to take together in terms of going for marriage counseling?

_____

Date you will take this step by:

_____

5. *Overcome barriers and fears.* Explain the steps you plan to take to overcome the barriers or fears you identified:

---

6. *Address faith struggles.* Name one step you plan to take to address your personal faith struggles or spiritual struggles you are experiencing as a couple:

Take Steps to Find a Therapist

If you're considering going to a therapist or medical provider, complete this section.

1. Describe the type of therapist or provider you need (individual, marriage, medication):

---

2. Review the steps above and locate and review several potential therapists:

---

3. Schedule a consultation and/or an in-person meeting and answer the following questions:

Do you feel comfortable with the therapist?

Do you think they can help you with your specific treatment needs?

4. If you answer yes to both questions, schedule a second appointment. If no, then meet a different therapist.

5. Evaluate your progress in five to six weeks.

Pray Together

Jesus, please provide us with friends, pastors, therapists, and doctors who can help support us in managing our stress together, strengthening our psychological health, and investing in our marriage. Help us to both work toward greater mental and emotional well-being, and please protect our minds and bodies. If marriage counseling would help us, please guide us to the right counselor. We know you are the center of our healing and recovery process. We are looking to you for direction and help. In Jesus's name, amen.

13

Cultivate Joy along the Trail

Gaining New Perspective on Your Journey

The joy of the LORD is your strength.

Nehemiah 8:10

We were soaking wet and shivering. The water kept coming at us, unrelenting wave after wave. It was so loud, with screams penetrating the air, that it was hard to concentrate. We kept getting hit in the face by objects flying at us from what seemed like all directions.

But we were laughing and smiling the whole time! On that cold spring day, we tossed balls with shrieks of joy as water splashed everyone. It was the opening day of our backyard pool.

About six weeks prior, we had started dreading the upcoming summer. It was the COVID-19 pandemic, and we couldn't travel that year because we couldn't risk our family's health by even going out to local places. Even the neighborhood pool was closed down for the year out of concern for people's safety. We could have been disappointed, but instead we came up with a plan to make our backyard a fun, memorable place. We honestly weren't looking forward to the effort needed to make it happen, but we all jumped in as a team and worked on it together. First, we fixed up our old swing set and added new features to it. Kristin scoured local websites to find a deal on some backyard furniture. Our son and Todd set to work on leveling the ground, hauling in sand, and assembling an above-ground pool. It felt like a monumental task to do by hand, and it took us a few weeks to get it all done. But we made wonderful memories as we talked, played in the dirt, and worked hard side by side, sharing this experience together.

So, the cold water that spring day didn't really matter because our hearts were warmed with joy. What truly put the smiles on our faces was seeing the culmination of our weeks of hard work and commitment. Our limitations faded away as we watched our kids laugh and play. We had been able to transform this challenging situation into a summer we could joyfully share together.

Learn to Live Joyfully

When asked about joy, most people will mention happiness. While they are similar, exploring the differences between the two will help us understand joy better. The root of happiness is an event or stimulus that triggers a positive emotional response in us. Something happens to us that makes us happy. Joy is different in that it comes from within and is not dependent on what's happening around or to us. Scripture teaches us to consider difficulties as "an opportunity for great joy" (James 1:2 NLT). Even when we are in the worst of situations, we can be joyful. Happiness is in the moment, but joy is deeper and longer lasting.

To cultivate a joyful life together, you must create a marriage environment that will nurture and produce joy and eliminate attitudes and reactions that prevent it. It takes steady work over a long period of time.

Each spouse may be at a different place in their ability to live joyfully, and it can be challenging to watch a spouse struggle. Living joyfully is a choice, and one spouse's joy can inspire and help the other through their struggles. We are called to lift one another up, and often our spouse can help us through our own worst times. Joy is contagious, and if one of you chooses joy, the overall joy in your marriage will likely grow.

Joy flourishes when there is space for it in our lives. If our hearts and minds are filled with other thoughts and negative feelings, there's no room for joy. Let's look at some practices that will help you grow a joyful life together and live joyfully in the present.

Change Your Perspective

Todd: Recently, Kristin and Bethany Grace came home from a full day at the ER. We were exhausted and just wanted to get Bethany Grace inside so we could start the long to-do list of putting her to bed. But Bethany Grace just stopped on the driveway and wouldn't come inside. I found myself impatient and frustrated because we had a lot to do. But as I paused and looked at her, I realized she was looking up. I followed her gaze and saw what she did—a beautiful night sky of twinkling stars. I looked up for a moment, and then I caught Kristin's eye. We both just watched Bethany Grace. Her eyes were lit up with awe and wonder. We felt a deep joy in our souls at the end of a long and worrisome day. If we had stuck to our determination to keep pushing to get it all done quickly, we would have missed out on this magical, joy-filled moment together.

The way we see a situation makes all the difference in our outlook on life and our overall mood. Maintaining optimism when facing struggles can be an important factor in our resilience and the quality of our life and marriage.[1] When we look for a positive way to view a difficult situation, we can persevere, and our marriage can grow and become stronger through our challenges and even tragedies. One of the most powerful ways to help find a new and positive perspective is to look back on your life together and the good things that have happened. Can you see God's love and provision? Can you see where events that didn't make sense at the time fit together for something special? Can you see where God transformed pain and sorrow into blessings and joy? We promise those gifts are there. Look for them and cherish them. Know that God is working on them all the time, and he will be right there beside you now and in the future with any challenges you face.

Enjoy Life's Little Blessings

If we can release some of our worries about the big details in our lives, we will have more time to notice and enjoy the amazing moments right around us. We'll begin to make meaning and learn that some of the most important and best memories in our lives revolve around small moments together. Bethany Grace's bedtime routine can take an hour or more sometimes. But we've learned to put aside our worries about what else has to be done and focus on the task of getting her to bed. We work together as a team, with one of us administering her tube feeding and medicines and the other helping with toileting and pajamas. We talk to each other and to Bethany Grace. We make up funny songs about the day or even joyfully sing about going potty. As we pass back and forth, we smile and make eye contact and even sneak in a quick kiss.

Most couples only get to enjoy the childhood bedtime routine for a few years. We know it's going to be part of our lives forever, so we slow down and just enjoy it together. Appreciating those little moments of joy and blessings in our daughter's room together are some of the best memories of our lives. They are different but just as meaningful as when we watched the Eiffel Tower lights twinkling at night or any other grand adventure we've been on together.

For you, maybe it's your time cooking or cleaning together. It can be waiting to collapse in bed at the exact same moment so you can both feel that relief of exhaustion as you look into each other's eyes and smile. Your shared commitment to sticking together and supporting one another even during the daily routines will draw you closer and make your life together more fun. Look for and plan those moments in your life, as they will be the memories that keep you going during the other hard times you face. These moments are like a warm glow inside that makes everything else better.

Celebrate Your Successes

If there is one thing that our daughter has taught us more than anything, it's that life is meant to be celebrated. A dry pull-up is a reason to jump for joy. A beautiful scribble deserves a high five. And it's okay to just stop in the middle of everything and have a dance party. We've tried to build that spirit into our everyday lives. We go all out for everybody's birthday. Our family celebrates finishing a race together, and we encourage each other every time one of us returns from a run. The two of us hug just because it's fun to see the other person. We do the Superman pose together after a good IEP meeting. We've even been known to let out a little yell of triumph after we tackle that big stack of dishes together. Sometimes we celebrate as a couple and a family—well, just because. Find ways to celebrate and have fun with the little things. The smiles and joy you share will carry over to all parts of your life.

Express Gratitude

If there was one easy practice you could do to make a drastic impact in your life and marriage, you would probably do it if it wasn't too hard, right? Well, expressing gratitude, thankfulness, and appreciation to each other is a simple practice that can:

Improve your physical and mental health.

Increase your resilience.

Foster more hope.

Lower psychological distress.

Build a stronger relationship.

Increase life satisfaction.

Enhance your intimacy.

Increase levels of forgiveness.

Help you cope more effectively.[2]

Expressing gratitude turns your focus to the positive aspects of your spouse and your marriage relationship, and when your spouse thanks you, you feel appreciated. This act creates good feelings between you and deepens your intimacy. This practice also fosters joy by increasing your positive emotions, even though the stressful circumstances haven't decreased. You look at life with an overall more positive attitude, which helps improve your physical and mental health. This is especially true when you thank God for each other and the blessings in your life, which gives you more hope. The way you perceive a situation changes as you realize how many blessings you already have in each other instead of focusing on what you don't have in your marriage. Gratitude helps you see you're not alone, and God and other people care about you.

Gratitude also helps build your marriage relationship, because your appreciation for each other shows that you are important to one another. Expressing gratitude to each other often elicits a positive response such as a smile or an affirming statement. This moment of connection builds more positive energy between you. It can set off a positive chain of events with one spouse joyfully trying to out-serve and out-thank the other.

Luckily, expressing gratitude is easy to do and can be as simple as completing one of these sentences:

"Thank you for . . ."

"I appreciate . . ."

"I'm grateful for . . ."

Start by trying one of these statements with each other at least once a day. We believe you will quickly see a difference in your marriage. You can then build on that momentum by trying some other ways of expressing gratitude. Think about what would be most meaningful for your partner and try it. Would it mean more to them if you told them in person, left them a note, or bragged on them in front of others? Here are a few ideas:

Write messages to each other on the mirror after your shower.

Send texts or videos thanking each other.

Hide little gifts of appreciation for each other, like a favorite candy bar.

Tape a blank "thankfulness paper" with a pen somewhere you can write spontaneous thank-you notes to each other.

Start a gratitude prayer notebook to write notes to each other and/or gratitude prayers to God for each other.

Most of all, be thankful to God, who blesses all our lives every day. When we see the ways he has blessed us, we are humbled and inspired to bless others. "Every good and perfect gift is from above, coming down from the Father of the heavenly lights, who does not change like shifting shadows" (James 1:17).

Choose a Life of Joy

It's been hard work, and you've had to choose to look at your marriage and life together differently. But the results have been life-changing. As you've worked through the previous chapters together, we hope you now feel a sense of renewal and energy as God continues to fill you with his goodness. You can see the challenges you've come through together, and you know the strength you've gained as a couple through those times. You trust each other more, as you know the other will always be there by your side. You love each other in ways you never imagined, and you care for one another in ways no one else can.

Celebrate the little successes and make a cake just because. Allow joy to well up in your soul to carry you through the hard days. No matter what may come, God has blessings for you right now, and you can find peace and joy in his presence and with one another. It doesn't mean your days are always going to be easy or happy. That's not what joy is. Joy is from within—from years of choices you've made, from the future you envision together, and through the ways you choose to live each day as you share this amazing journey together.

Build the Skills

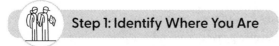 **Step 1: Identify Where You Are**

1. How would you define joy?

Wife:

_____

Husband:

_____

2. What are some examples of joy in your life?

Wife:

_____

Husband:

_____

_____

Share these with each other!

3. How would you rate yourself on living "joyfully in the present" in each of the areas we explored?

Having a positive perspective.

Wife:

| Poor | Fair | Good | Great | Superstar |

Husband:

| Poor | Fair | Good | Great | Superstar |

Enjoying life's little blessings.

Wife:

| Poor | Fair | Good | Great | Superstar |

Husband:

| Poor | Fair | Good | Great | Superstar |

Celebrating everyday successes.

Wife:

| Poor | Fair | Good | Great | Superstar |

Husband:

| Poor | Fair | Good | Great | Superstar |

Expressing gratitude to your spouse.

Wife:

Poor	Fair	Good	Great	Superstar

Husband:

Poor	Fair	Good	Great	Superstar

Expressing gratitude to God.

Wife:

Poor	Fair	Good	Great	Superstar

Husband:

Poor	Fair	Good	Great	Superstar

 Step 2: Set Your Goal

Pick one of the ways to live joyfully in the present and write a goal for it.

Wife:

_____

_____

Husband:

_____

_____

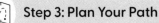 **Step 3: Plan Your Path**

Write out the specific ways you will work on one of the practices that builds joy (having a positive perspective, enjoying life's little blessings, celebrating everyday successes, expressing gratitude to your spouse, expressing gratitude to God).

Wife:

_____

_____

_____

Husband:

_____

_____

_____

──────────────── **Pray Together** ────────────────

God, you are the source of all good and joy in our world. We want to focus on you more and on all the little blessings you have placed in our life together. Fill us with gratitude and a spirit of celebration. Change our perspective on life so that we can see our purpose through your eyes. Then we will be able to better see the good all around us and the ways you are already working in our life and marriage. Help us to choose joy each day. In Jesus's name, amen.

Conclusion

Envision Your Path Ahead

See, I am doing a new thing! Now it springs up; do you not perceive it? I am making a way in the wilderness and streams in the wasteland.

Isaiah 43:19

We've compared the challenges you're facing in your marriage to trekking on a difficult wilderness expedition. At the start of your journey, it was all you could do just to survive together. Hopefully at this point you've begun developing additional marriage skills, and you've been able to move beyond the day-to-day crisis mode. Life is more manageable now, and your marriage is doing better or maybe even great. It can be easy to settle into this comfortable stage in your life and relationship. There's nothing wrong with simply enjoying this season. Yet we want to challenge you to go a little further. With the foundation you have now built, your marriage can grow even stronger. But you must intentionally continue to develop these skills, invest time in your relationship, and plan your future together.

During our yearlong graduate school internship, we were required to go on a winter camping trip in the wilderness of the Upper Peninsula of Michigan. Being from the South, we had never experienced that much snow or bitter temperatures down to twenty degrees below zero. We knew we couldn't just go on a trip like that without a lot of careful planning and developing some advanced skills. When we began the program, we didn't have the basic skills to even think about attempting this kind of adventure. But over the course of a couple of months, we learned how to layer our clothes for subzero temperatures, snowshoe, wax our cross-country skis, and build a fire with sticks buried several feet beneath the snow. We even learned how to build an igloo-like hut called a quinzhee.

We finally felt like we had honed our skills and could survive for multiple nights out in the frozen wilderness. It was time to plan that camping trip. We looked at maps and trailheads for potential sites. We talked through logistics with one another and with our leaders. We made some pretty audacious plans. We were going to cross-country ski all the way to Lake Superior!

We'd never dreamed about doing anything like this before. But there we were, just a couple of hours' driving distance from the trailhead to Lake Superior. If everything went just right, we would have the chance to experience a view that very few people in the world ever get to see. Sure, we could have chosen to just stay in the safety and comfort of our cozy home, but this opportunity was hard to pass up.

Lake Superior was too far for us to ski to in one day, so we skied about halfway and began putting our skills to the test by building our quinzhee, making a fire, and setting up base camp. It took the rest of the day, and we were worn out when we climbed into our frozen cave for the night. We needed a good night's sleep because tomorrow's journey was going to be long and difficult. We would need to set out very early to make it to the lakeshore by dusk, as we would need to ski all the way back to camp before it became too cold to be out in the elements. We knew we might end up having to turn around and head back to our base camp before reaching our destination, but we decided it was worth the try.

After a long and cold night, we set out on the adventure together. As we began gliding through the peaceful woods, we felt like we were in a different world. The snow made a pristine white landscape and muted all other sounds so that we could hear only each other and our skis trekking through the snow. We started out joyfully, anticipating our destination, but the daylong excursion soon became grueling and exhausting. Falls, bruises, protesting arms, and aching legs made us wonder what could possibly make this trip worth it. As we neared late afternoon, we were less sure we would reach our destination.

Then, the trees parted into a clearing up ahead. As we coasted downhill around a corner, a hint of our destination peeked through the trees. The sun was just beginning to rest on the surface of the lake. Tropical shades of pinks, yellows, and oranges seemed to burst up out of the water into the sky. We skied faster, forgetting our fatigue. We stopped when we reached a sharp ledge with a forty-foot drop into icy water below. Peering down, we watched a churning mass of blue and white icebergs floating in partially frozen water. We felt a sense of great danger but also indescribable wonder. Into the far distance, endless dark-blue water rolled. Awestruck, we witnessed a magnificent sunset unfold until the blood-orange globe had fully melted into the water. One of the most challenging undertakings of our marriage and lives led us to a rare event that very few people ever witness.

Like that winter wilderness trip, your journey to strengthen your marriage while caring for your child with special needs has probably felt grueling, terrifying, and exhausting at times. But take a moment to look around and see where you are and how far you've come as a couple. Sure, there will still be hard days ahead, and you'll always be growing, but now you can start to plan out where you would like to go together and what stops you'd like to enjoy along the way. Now you can venture out beyond your base camp and reach for those dreams you never thought were possible. When you have a destination you are working toward, the journey becomes so much more meaningful. Making specific plans together has given us something special to look forward to and has made even the most challenging days feel lighter.

Now that you've worked together to begin building the skills and stabilizing your relationship and daily life, you can pull out the "not right now" box from chapter 3. What's one of your dreams or goals you had for your marriage that you can now plan together? Maybe it's a relationship goal like building deeper trust or a closer friendship. Maybe it's enjoying an activity or hobby together, starting a business or working together, taking a special trip together, growing spiritually together, or volunteering or serving in ministry together. It can be anything that will strengthen your marriage and give you enjoyable time together. Your shared dream can draw you closer together around a common goal that is inclusive of your child but goes beyond your role as caregivers. This process will challenge the two of you to look at your own values, your dreams, and how God has made you.

So, what will be your marriage story? Look ahead at the trail before you. If you could paint a dream future path together, what would it look like? Envision happy and fun years ahead. Dreaming and planning will help build your long-term relationship health and success. If you can find even a small amount of hope and joy in your marriage, you can weather the most difficult path and worst storm and continue to grow closer to each other.

Yes, you are still in the wilderness, and you will always need to proceed with caution and intentionally nurture your relationship. But now you can begin to plan and dream together about how you desire your life together to look. You've discovered a deeper sense of love and vulnerability than most "typical" couples ever experience or can understand. This journey is difficult and not what you expected or hoped for, yet by persevering together through your loss and challenges, you've discovered deeper intimacy, richer meaning, and greater strength in your marriage.

Your future together can be better than you ever imagined. You can't know what lies ahead on your path, but you can walk toward and look for a hopeful and joyful future together, shining on the horizon just around the bend.

Set a New Bearing

Here is your final exercise: planning your ideal future together.

1. Describe one meaningful marriage experience from the past year beyond your role as caregivers—maybe a meal you enjoyed, a visit to a new place, or an intimate moment you shared:

---

2. List one or two strengths of your marriage outside of your role as parents:

---

3. Look through the sticky notes you put away in the box in chapter 3 and brainstorm about other new, specific goals you might have as a couple. Refer back to the list of examples to spark ideas. Or share a goal or dream with your spouse you have kept to yourself until now. Don't think about the logistics. Just be a couple and dream together. You will plan the practical steps to achieving your dream soon enough. But for now, just have fun thinking about the future possibilities.

List every idea you come up with:

_____

_____

_____

_____

4. **Choose one** future dream or goal you share for your relationship:

_____

_____

5. Brainstorm the concrete steps you'll need to take for your dream to become a reality:

_____

_____

_____

_____

6. Talk about how you can begin to work on each step:

_____

_____

_____

_____

7. Set a date for when you would like to start or make your dream a reality.

Date: _____

8. Set a date for when you will assess your planning progress (about halfway to your goal date). Make this time fun and do it as a night out, or take off for a day to have lunch while you evaluate.

Date: _____

Get Going!

Commit to trying to make your dream a reality. What first step will you take and when? Maybe it could even be this week!

Step: _____

When: _____

Pray Together

Father God, we know you hold our future together and are preparing joyful blessings ahead. You promise us in Jeremiah 29:11 that you have good plans for us, "plans to prosper [us] and not to harm [us], plans to give [us] hope and a future." Help us to trust in you to guide us and to provide for all our needs. As we work toward planning our dream together, help make it a reality by providing the resources and support we need. Thank you for how you are healing and strengthening our marriage. Please continue to grow our relationship as we rely on you. In Jesus's name, amen.

Disability Parenting Marriage Assessment Tool

This assessment is meant to be done individually by each spouse. You can make copies and do it at the same time or take turns recording your answers. Allow five to ten minutes to choose your immediate thoughts on each question. Don't try to solve anything right now or worry about your answers. Just get your thoughts down on paper so you can use them later, on your journey with us. Take a deep breath, then slowly exhale. Without getting bogged down, briefly examine these different areas of your marriage.

Wife Questionnaire

Overall, how would you rate the current health of your marriage?

Poor	Fair	Good	Great	Excellent

Stress Levels

1. How would you rate the current stress level between you and your spouse?

Very low	Low	Moderate	High	Very high

2. How would you rate your stress level due to situational issues you are facing together in caring for your child and family?

Very low	Low	Moderate	High	Very high

3. Is stress about any of these areas creating strain on your relationship? (Circle all that apply.)

Your child's symptoms

Your child's behaviors

Your child's care needs

Finances

Housing

School

Employment

Completing day-to-day responsibilities

Hospitalizations

Other stressors: _____

4. How would you say the two of you do at managing parenting stress together?

Not at all well	Not so well	Okay	Very well

Overall, how would you rate your levels of stress?

Poor	Fair	Good	Great	Excellent

Communication and Emotional Intimacy

1. How strong is your emotional connection?

Not present at all	Not so strong	Somewhat strong	Strong	Very strong

2. Do you feel like you can safely share your thoughts and feelings with your spouse?

Yes	No	Sometimes

3. How well do you communicate?

Not very well	Somewhat well	Well	Very well

4. Do you believe you support your spouse emotionally?

Yes	No

5. Have you been able to grieve your loss together?

Yes, a lot	Yes, some	Not really	Not at all

6. Have you and/or your spouse withdrawn emotionally?

Yes	No

7. How often do you dream together or talk about career or intellectual interests?

Not at all	Not very often	Sometimes	Somewhat often	Often

8. How often do you argue?

Not at all	Not very often	Sometimes	Somewhat often	Often

9. How well do you solve problems together?

Not very well	Somewhat well	Well	Very well

Overall, how would you rate your communication and emotional connection?

Poor	Fair	Good	Great	Excellent

Physical Intimacy

1. Have you been able to stay close physically?

Yes	No

2. Do you regularly show affection like hugging, holding hands, snuggling, and kissing?

Yes	No

3. How much alone time do you have together?

None	Five minutes occasionally	Short blocks of 1–2 hours	Extended periods

4. Do you often find yourself physically tired?

Yes	No

5. How often do you enjoy sexual intimacy?

1–2 times/week	1–2 times/month	1–2 times/ 4 months	Other

Overall, how would you rate your physical intimacy?

Poor	Fair	Good	Great	Excellent

Faith

1. Are you on the same path in your faith?

Yes	No

2. Are either or both of you struggling with spiritual questions or doubts?

Yes	No

3. Is your reliance on your faith a strength in your marriage?

Yes	No

4. Does the topic of faith cause any conflict in your relationship?

Yes	No

5. Do you worship together?

Yes	No

Overall, how would you rate your faith?

Poor	Fair	Good	Great	Excellent

Social Support

What is the level of support you receive from the following groups?

1. Family and friends

Low	Moderate	High

2. Other disability parents

Low	Moderate	High

3. A support group

Low	Moderate	High

4. A church community

Low	Moderate	High

Overall, how would you rate your level of social support?

Poor	Fair	Good	Great	Excellent

Finances and Other Resources

1. Do you currently feel stressed about your finances?

Yes	No

2. Are you utilizing national, state, local, or other resources and programs?

Yes	No

3. Are you worried about your financial future?

Yes	No

Overall, how would you rate your level of financial health?

Poor	Fair	Good	Great	Excellent

Husband Questionnaire

Overall, how would you rate the current health of your marriage?

Poor	Fair	Good	Great	Excellent

Stress Levels

1. How would you rate the current stress level between you and your spouse?

Very low	Low	Moderate	High	Very high

2. How would you rate your stress level due to situational issues you are facing together in caring for your child and family?

Very low	Low	Moderate	High	Very high

3. Is stress about any of these areas creating strain on your relationship? (Circle all that apply.)

    Your child's symptoms
    Your child's behaviors
    Your child's care needs
    Finances
    Housing
    School
    Employment
    Completing day-to-day responsibilities
    Hospitalizations
    Other stressors: _____

4. How would you say the two of you do at managing parenting stress together?

Not at all well	Not so well	Okay	Very well

Overall, how would you rate your levels of stress?

Poor	Fair	Good	Great	Excellent

Communication and Emotional Intimacy

1. How strong is your emotional connection?

Not present at all	Not so strong	Somewhat strong	Strong	Very strong

2. Do you feel like you can safely share your thoughts and feelings with your spouse?

Yes	No	Sometimes

3. How well do you communicate?

Not very well	Somewhat well	Well	Very well

4. Do you believe you support your spouse emotionally?

Yes	No

5. Have you been able to grieve your loss together?

Yes, a lot	Yes, some	Not really	Not at all

6. Have you and/or your spouse withdrawn emotionally?

Yes	No

7. How often do you dream together or talk about career or intellectual interests?

Not at all	Not very often	Sometimes	Somewhat often	Often

8. How often do you argue?

Not at all	Not very often	Sometimes	Somewhat often	Often

9. How well do you solve problems together?

Not very well	Somewhat well	Well	Very well

Overall, how would you rate your communication and emotional connection?

Poor	Fair	Good	Great	Excellent

Physical Intimacy

1. Have you been able to stay close physically?

Yes	No

2. Do you regularly show affection like hugging, holding hands, snuggling, and kissing?

Yes	No

3. How much alone time do you have together?

None	Five minutes occasionally	Short blocks of 1–2 hours	Extended periods

4. Do you often find yourself physically tired?

Yes	No

5. How often do you enjoy sexual intimacy?

1–2 times/week	1–2 times/month	1–2 times/ 4 months	Other

Overall, how would you rate your physical intimacy?

Poor	Fair	Good	Great	Excellent

Faith

1. Are you on the same path in your faith?

Yes	No

2. Are either or both of you struggling with spiritual questions or doubts?

Yes	No

3. Is your reliance on your faith a strength in your marriage?

Yes	No

4. Does the topic of faith cause any conflict in your relationship?

Yes	No

5. Do you worship together?

Yes	No

Overall, how would you rate your faith?

Poor	Fair	Good	Great	Excellent

Social Support

What is the level of support you receive from the following groups?

1. Family and friends

Low	Moderate	High

2. Other disability parents

Low	Moderate	High

3. A support group

Low	Moderate	High

4. A church community

Low	Moderate	High

Overall, how would you rate your level of social support?

Poor	Fair	Good	Great	Excellent

Finances and Other Resources

1. Do you currently feel stressed about your finances?

Yes	No

2. Are you utilizing national, state, local, or other resources and programs?

Yes	No

3. Are you worried about your financial future?

Yes	No

Overall, how would you rate your level of financial health?

Poor	Fair	Good	Great	Excellent

Assessment Summary

Record your overall rating from above for each of the following areas of your marriage. These questions are at the end of each section and begin with the word **Overall**.

Here are the corresponding scores to give each answer choice next to your response.

Poor: 1	Fair: 2	Good: 3	Great: 4	Excellent: 5

Overall Initial Rating (First Question)

Wife's Score ____

Husband's Score ____

Stress Levels

Wife's Score ____

Husband's Score ____

Communication and Emotional Intimacy

Wife's Score ____

Husband's Score ____

Physical Intimacy

Wife's Score ____

Husband's Score ____

Faith

Wife's Score ____

Husband's Score ____

Social Support

Wife's Score ____

Husband's Score ____

Finances and Other Resources

Wife's Score ____

Husband's Score ____

Total _____

Overall Score Results

55 or More: Great to Excellent

Your marriage is in an incredible place. You must have worked very hard and are probably years into your journey. In fact, you seriously should consider finding another set of disability parents, giving them this book, and mentoring them. Practice the skills in each chapter to continue to enhance every area of your marriage.

35–54: Good

You're doing okay. Some areas of your marriage are likely stronger and others more vulnerable. Build on your strengths and practice the skills in each chapter to continue to strengthen all the different areas of your relationship.

34 or Less: Fair to Poor

If we had taken this assessment ourselves a year after becoming disability parents, this is probably where we would have ranked. So, the great news is that there is hope. With hard work, practicing the skills in each chapter, prayer, and commitment, you can grow a stronger marriage than you ever dreamed.

Your specific score is just a reflection of the current state of your marriage. If one or both of you had a low overall score, don't despair. Like anything in life, if you work on it, it will likely get better. If you ignore your marriage, it will get worse. It seems many couples get so wrapped up in the caregiving and demands of life that they never take the time to assess the health of their marriage. This assessment is meant to help you see the strengths in your relationship and also realize those areas that need extra attention.

The only way to improve your marriage is to acknowledge your weaknesses and challenges. Then, you can take the first step on your journey to a stronger marriage. We are confident that if you journey with us through this book and complete the exercises, you will experience positive changes in your marriage and life! We encourage you to complete this assessment again after you have worked through the exercises at the end of each chapter. Then you will see the fruits of your labor and all the ways that God is transforming your marriage.

Resources

As promised, we've collected a good amount of additional resources for you to help you along your journey. Utilizing these supports can help you reduce your overall stress level and save you time and money. We have used a lot of these resources ourselves, and we hope you will check into how they can support your marriage and family too.

Todd and Kristin

Chapter 3 Repack Your Packs

Stephen R. Covey, 7 *Habits of Highly Effective Families: Creating a Nurturing Family in a Turbulent World*, revised and updated edition (New York: St. Martin's, 2022).

Terri Mauro, "10 Ways to Help Your Family Get Organized," Friendship Circle, January 8, 2017, https://www.friendshipcircle.org/blog/2017/01/09/10-ways-to-help-your-family-get-organized-for-2017.

Erica Goodwin, The Pediatric Special Needs Toolkit (planner and organizer), Competent Caregiver (Etsy shop), https://www.etsy.com/listing/1302897515/pediatric-special-needs-toolkit-planner?.

Chapter 4 Cope as a Couple

Pull out a card from one of the following decks and practice the short exercise together.

Matthew McKay and Jeffrey C. Wood, *The Dialectical Behavior Therapy Skills Card Deck: 52 Practices to Balance Your Emotions Every Day* (Oakland, CA: New Harbinger, 2019).

Bob Stahl and Elisha Goldstein, *A Mindfulness-Based Stress Reduction Card Deck* (Oakland, CA: New Harbinger, 2021).

Chapter 6 Tackle Problems Together

Health Care, Home Health, and Prescriptions

Kids' Waivers (information on children's Medicaid waivers, Katie Beckett programs, and other Medicaid programs), https://www.kidswaivers.org/.

"The National Resource Center for Rx Assistance Plans" (assistance plans by state), https://www.staterxplans.us/.

Asthma and Allergy Foundation of America, "Drug Assistance Program" (medication cost assistance programs), https://aafa.org/advocacy/advocacy-resources/patient-assistance-medicine-drug-programs/.

Advocacy

Family Voices, https://familyvoices.org/.

The Arc, https://thearc.org/.

Center for Parent Information & Resources, "Find Your Parent Center" (parent training by state), https://www.parentcenterhub.org/find-your-center/.

Social Security Administration, "Check Eligibility for Social Security Benefits" (for your child), https://www.ssa.gov/prepare/check-eligibility-for-benefits.

Centers for Disease Control and Prevention (CDC), "Learn the Signs. Act Early.: Information by State" (early intervention services; free therapies and services for under age three), https://www.cdc.gov/ncbddd/actearly/parents/state-text.html.

Special Olympics, https://www.specialolympics.org/.

Equipment Exchange Programs Locator, https://www.rifton.com/adaptive-mobility-blog/blog-posts/2013/may/lending-libraries-loan-closets.

United Cerebral Palsy (check your local foundation to inquire about equipment exchange programs), https://ucp.org/find-us/.

Chapter 8 Stop to Rest Together

ARCH National Respite Network and Resource Center, "Find a Respite Provider: National Respite Locator Service" (respite coalitions and grants), https://archrespite.org/caregiver-resources/respitelocator/.

Jill's House (overnight care), https://www.jillshouse.org/.

Nathaniel's Hope, "Buddy Break," https://nathanielshope.org/our-programs/buddy-break/.

99balloons, "rEcess: A Night of Respite," https://99balloons.org/recess/.

United Cerebral Palsy, "Parents and Families," https://ucp.org/resource-guide/parents-and-families/.

Easter Seals, "Respite Services Profile," https://www.easterseals.com/programs-and-services/camping-recreation/respite-services-profile.html.

Easter Seals, "Camp and Recreation Directory," https://www.easterseals.com/programs-and-services/camping-recreation/camp-and-recreation-directory.html.

Very Special Camps, "Summer Camps & Programs for Individuals with Special Needs," https://www.veryspecialcamps.com/.

The Mighty, "Summer Camps for Kids with Disabilities You May Want to Check Out," https://themighty.com/topic/disability/summer-camps-kids-teens-adults-disabilities/.

Friendship Circle, "25 Summer Camps for Individuals with Special Needs," https://www.friendshipcircle.org/blog/2013/02/13/25-summer-camps-for-individuals-with-special-needs.

Chapter 9 Enjoy One Another on the Journey

Sheila Wray Gregoire, *31 Days to Great Sex: Love. Friendship. Fun.* (Winnipeg, MB: Word Alive, 2013).

Clifford Penner and Joyce J. Penner, *The Gift of Sex: A Guide to Sexual Fulfillment* (Nashville: Nelson, 2003).

Ed Wheat and Gaye Wheat, *Intended for Pleasure*, fourth edition (Grand Rapids: Revell, 2010).

Chapter 10 Find Others to Travel Beside

Key Ministry, "Find a Church" (find a church with a disability ministry), https://www.keyministry.org/find-a-church.

Ability Ministry, "Disability Ministry Locator," https://abilityministry.com/disability-ministry-locator/.

Rising Above Ministries (online Bible study, community groups, and retreats for couples, moms, and dads), https://www.risingabovemin istries.org/.

Walk Right In Ministries, "Peer Discussion Groups" (online Christian community for parent caregivers), https://walkrightin.org/services /peer-discussion-groups/.

Joni & Friends, "Retreats & Getaways" (parent, family, and marriage retreats and getaways), https://www.joniandfriends.org/ministries /retreats-and-getaways/.

Wonderfully Made Family Camp, https://wonderfullymadecamp.org/.

Parent to Parent USA (peer support from other parent caregivers), https://www.p2pusa.org/.

Chapter 11 Have One Another's Backs

Centers for Disease Control and Prevention (CDC), "Learn the Signs. Act Early.: Concerned about Your Child's Development?" https:// www.cdc.gov/ncbddd/actearly/concerned.html/#childthree.

Mark Bertin and Ari Tuckman, *Mindful Parenting for ADHD: A Guide to Cultivating Calm, Reducing Stress, and Helping Children Thrive* (A New Harbinger Self-Help Workbook) (Oakland, CA: New Harbinger, 2015).

Nicole Libin, *Mindful Parenting in a Chaotic World: Effective Strategies to Stay Centered At Home and On the Go* (Emeryville, CA: Rockridge Press, 2019).

Chapter 12 Call Out for Help

Christian Counselor Directory, "Find a Christian Therapist: In-Person or Virtual," https://www.christiancounselordirectory.com/.

Psychology Today, "Find a Therapist" (you can narrow the search with choices like "marriage counseling" and "Christian counselors"), https://www.psychologytoday.com/us/therapists.

Amanda Griffith Atkins, "Therapist Directory" (directory for therapists experienced in working with families with disabilities), https:// www.amandagriffithatkins.com/therapist-directory.

National Institute of Mental Health (NIMH), "My Mental Health: Do I Need Help?," https://www.nimh.nih.gov/health/publications/my -mental-health-do-i-need-help.

National Institute of Mental Health (NIMH), "Post-Traumatic Stress Disorder," https://www.nimh.nih.gov/health/topics/post-traumatic -stress-disorder-ptsd.

National Alliance on Mental Illness (NAMI), "NAMI Family Support Group," https://nami.org/Support-Education/Support-Groups /NAMI-Family-Support-Group.

National Alliance on Mental Illness (NAMI), "Supporting Recovery," https://nami.org/Your-Journey/Family-Members-and-Caregivers /Supporting-Recovery.

Substance Abuse and Mental Health Services Administration (SAMHSA), "How to Help Someone You Care About," https:// www.samhsa.gov/find-support/helping-someone.

Cleveland Clinic, "5 Ways to Offer Support When Your Spouse Is Depressed," https://health.clevelandclinic.org/5-ways-to-offer-support -when-your-spouse-is-depressed/.

Acknowledgments

Without the love and support of our family and friends, creating this book would not have been possible.

To our two precious and rare children: Thank you for giving us the gift of being your parents and having the privilege of loving and caring for you.

To Kristin's mom and dad, Mary Lou and Randy: Thank you for believing in us and this book and for spending sometimes more days at our home than your own helping care for the children and the housework so we could work on the book. Most of all, we are forever grateful for your never-ending love and support that have helped keep our marriage and family strong through some very challenging years. In addition, Randy, we greatly appreciate you laboring to read through the manuscript twice, double-checking Scripture citations and giving us numerous editing suggestions.

To Todd's dad, Les: Thank you for your sacrificial love and service. You have taken care of so many things in the business so we could have time to write. We are incredibly grateful for all the times you watched the kids so we could get away to build our marriage.

To Todd's mom, Sherrie: Though you barely got to know your two grandchildren, as ALS took you away too soon, your legacy of love and care live on in this book and in us.

To our closest friends who never left our side even during our darkest times: We are grateful beyond words for your unconditional love and support.

To Dr. Scottie May, Dr. S. Steven Kang, and all our professors at Wheaton College: Thank you for helping us see the world in new ways and for shaping our views on ministry and serving others with the love of Christ.

To our editor, Rachel Freire O'Connor, and the entire Baker team: Thank you for believing in this book and diligently working to get it into the hands of couples who desperately need it.

To our agent, Steven Hutson: Thank you for believing in our ministry and vision for this book.

Thank you all.

Notes

Chapter 1 Survey Your Surroundings

1. Brian H. Freedman et al., "Relationship Status among Parents of Children with Autism Spectrum Disorders: A Population-Based Study," *Journal of Autism and Developmental Disorders* 42 (April 2012): 539–48, https://doi.org/10.1007/s10803-011-1269-y.

2. Shailender Swaminathan, Greg R. Alexander, and Sheree Boulet, "Delivering a Very Low Birth Weight Infant and the Subsequent Risk of Divorce or Separation," *Maternal and Child Health Journal* 10 (November 2006): 473–79, https://doi.org/10.1007/s10995-006-0146-3; Sigan L. Hartley et al., "Couple Conflict in Parents of Children with versus without Autism: Self-Reported and Observed Findings," *Journal of Child and Family Studies* 26, no. 8 (August 2017): 2152–65, https://doi.org/10.1007/s10826-017-0737-1.

3. Don Risdal and George H. Singer, "Marital Adjustment in Parents of Children with Disabilities: A Historical Review and Meta-Analysis," *Research & Practice for Persons with Severe Disabilities* 29, no. 2 (2004): 95–103, https://doi.org/10.2511/rpsd.29.2.95; Julie L. Ramisch, Esther Onaga, and Su Min Oh, "Keeping a Sound Marriage: How Couples with Children with Autism Spectrum Disorders Maintain Their Marriages," *Journal of Child and Family Studies* 23 (August 2014): 975–88, https://doi.org/10.1007/s10826-013-9753-y.

4. David McConnell and Amber Savage, "Stress and Resilience among Families Caring for Children with Intellectual Disability: Expanding the Research Agenda," *Current Developmental Disorders Reports* 2 (June 2015): 100–109, https://doi.org/10.1007/s40474-015-0040-z; Linda M. Raffaele Mendez et al., "Fostering Resilience among Couples Coparenting a Young Child with Autism: An Evaluation of *Together We Are Stronger*," *The American Journal of Family Therapy* 47, no. 3 (2019): 165–82, https://doi.org/10.1080/01926187.2019.1624225.

5. Jamie C. Brehaut et al., "Using Canadian Administrative Health Data to Examine the Health of Caregivers of Children with and without Health Problems: A

Demonstration of Feasibility," *International Journal of Population Data Science* 4, no. 1 (April 2019): 1–10, https://doi.org/10.23889/ijpds.v4i1.584; Lucyna M. Lach et al., "The Health and Psychosocial Functioning of Caregivers of Children with Neurodevelopmental Disorders," *Disability and Rehabilitation* 31, no. 8 (July 2009): 607–18, https://doi.org/10.1080/09638280802242163.

6. Angela Paster, David Brandwein, and Joanne Walsh, "A Comparison of Coping Strategies Used by Parents of Children with Disabilities and Parents of Children without Disabilities," *Research in Developmental Disabilities* 30, no. 6 (November–December 2009): 1337–42, https://doi.org/10.1016/j.ridd.2009.05.010.

Chapter 2 Embrace Your Unexpected Journey

1. P. R. Ujianti, "The Role of Support Group for Parents of Children with Special Needs," *Journal of Psychology and Instruction* 2, no. 1 (2018): 31–37, https://doi.org/10.23887/jpai.v2i1.13739.

2. Marsha M. Linehan, *DBT Skills Training Handouts and Worksheets*, 2nd ed. (New York: Guilford Press, 2015), 342.

3. Nikko S. Da Paz et al., "Acceptance or Despair?: Maternal Adjustment to Having a Child Diagnosed with Autism," *Journal of Autism and Developmental Disorders* 48, no. 6 (June 2018): 1971–81, https://doi.org/10.1007/s10803-017 -3450-4.

4. Manuel Fernández-Alcántara et al., "Feelings of Loss and Grief in Parents of Children Diagnosed with Autism Spectrum Disorder (ASD)," *Research in Developmental Disabilities* 55 (August 2016): 312–21, https://doi.org/10.1016 /j.ridd.2016.05.007.

5. Da Paz et al., "Acceptance or Despair?," 1971.

6. McConnell and Savage, "Stress and Resilience among Families Caring for Children with Intellectual Disability," 104.

7. Lori L. Batchelor and Gloria Duke, "Chronic Sorrow in Parents with Chronically Ill Children," *Pediatric Nursing* 45, no. 4 (July–August 2019): 163–83; Douglas Barnett et al., "Building New Dreams: Supporting Parents' Adaptation to Their Child with Special Needs," *Infants and Young Children* 16, no. 3 (July 2003): 184–200.

Chapter 3 Repack Your Packs

1. Sesen Negash et al., "Intimacy in the Midst of Caregiving: Examining Relationship and Sexual Satisfaction of Parents Raising Children with Special Needs," *Journal of Family Psychotherapy* 26, no. 3 (July 2015): 190–209, https://doi.org/10 .1080/08975353.2015.1067532; Diane Pelchat, Hélène Lefebvre, and Marie-Josée Levert, "Gender Differences and Similarities in the Experience of Parenting a Child with a Health Problem: Current State of Knowledge," *Journal of Child Health Care* 11, no. 2 (June 2007): 112–31, https://doi.org/10.1177/136749350707 6064.

2. Negash et al., "Intimacy in the Midst of Caregiving," 191–93; Debra Meleski, "Families with Chronically Ill Children: A Literature Review Examines Approaches to Helping Them Cope," *American Journal of Nursing* 102, no. 5 (May 2002): 47–54.

3. Justin W. Peer and Stephen B. Hillman, "Stress and Resilience for Parents of Children with Intellectual and Developmental Disabilities: A Review of Key Factors and Recommendations for Practitioners," *Journal of Policy and Practice in Intellectual Disabilities* 11, no. 2 (June 2014): 92–98, https://doi.org/10.1111/jppi.12072.

4. Negash et al., "Intimacy in the Midst of Caregiving," 193.

5. Elaine E. MacDonald and Richard P. Hastings, "Mindful Parenting and Care Involvement of Fathers of Children with Intellectual Disabilities," *Journal of Child and Family Studies* 19 (April 2010): 236–40, https://doi.org/10.1007/s10826-008-9243-9; Jake Johnson and Fred P. Piercy, "Exploring Partner Intimacy among Couples Raising Children on the Autism Spectrum: A Grounded Theory Investigation," *Journal of Marital and Family Therapy* 43, no. 4 (October 2017): 644–61, https://doi.org/10.1111/jmft.12247.

6. John M. Gottman and Nan Silver, *The Seven Principles for Making Marriage Work* (New York: Harmony Books, 2015), 214.

7. McConnell and Savage, "Stress and Resilience among Families Caring for Children with Intellectual Disability," 104–5.

Chapter 4 Cope as a Couple

1. T. Holmberg Bergman et al., "Acceptance and Commitment Therapy Group Intervention for Parents of Children with Disabilities (Navigator ACT): An Open Feasibility Trial," *Journal of Autism and Developmental Disorders* 53, no. 5 (May 2023): 1834–49, https://doi.org/10.1007/s10803-022-05490-6; Peer and Hillman, "Stress and Resilience for Parents of Children with Intellectual and Developmental Disabilities," 94.

2. Merideth Robinson and Cameron L. Neece, "Marital Satisfaction, Parental Stress, and Child Behavior Problems among Parents of Young Children with Developmental Disabilities," *Journal of Mental Health Research in Intellectual Disabilities* 8, no. 1 (2015): 23–46, https://doi.org/10.1080/19315864.2014.994247; Ramisch, Onaga, and Min Oh, "Keeping a Sound Marriage," 975–76.

3. Angela Sim et al., "Relationship Satisfaction and Dyadic Coping in Couples with a Child with Autism Spectrum Disorder," *Journal of Autism and Developmental Disorders* 47, no. 11 (November 2017): 3562–73, https://doi.org/10.1007/s10803-017-3275-1.

4. Gyeong-A. Park and Oan Na Lee, "The Moderating Effect of Social Support on Parental Stress and Depression in Mothers of Children with Disabilities," *Occupational Therapy International* 2022 (March 2022): 1–8, https://doi.org/10.1155/2022/5162954; Johnson and Piercy, "Exploring Partner Intimacy among Couples Raising Children on the Autism Spectrum," 644.

5. Park and Lee, "Moderating Effect of Social Support on Parental Stress and Depression in Mothers of Children with Disabilities," 1–2; Alicia Bazzano et al., "Mindfulness Based Stress Reduction (MBSR) for Parents and Caregivers of Individuals with Developmental Disabilities: A Community-Based Approach," *Journal of Child and Family Studies* 24 (February 2015): 298–308, https://doi.org/10.1007/s10826-013-9836-9.

6. Sugandha Sharma, Radhakrishnan Govindan, and J. V. S. Kommu, "Effectiveness of Parent-to-Parent Support Group in Reduction of Anxiety and Stress among Parents of Children with Autism and Attention Deficit Hyperactivity Disorder," *Indian Journal of Psychological Medicine* 44, no. 6 (November 2022): 575–79, https://doi.org/10.1177/02537176211072984; Bergman et al., "Acceptance and Commitment Therapy Group Intervention for Parents of Children with Disabilities (Navigator ACT)," 1834.

7. Paster, Brandwein, and Walsh, "Comparison of Coping Strategies Used by Parents of Children with Disabilities and Parents of Children without Disabilities," 1341.

8. Larissa G. Duncan, J. D. Coatsworth, and Mark T. Greenberg, "A Model of Mindful Parenting: Implications for Parent-Child Relationships and Prevention Research," *Clinical Child and Family Psychology Review* 12, no. 3 (September 2009): 255–70, https://doi.org/10.1007/s10567-009-0046-3.

9. Barnett et al., "Building New Dreams," 185; Negash et al., "Intimacy in the Midst of Caregiving," 192, 200.

10. Negash et al., "Intimacy in the Midst of Caregiving," 201; Sim et al., "Relationship Satisfaction and Dyadic Coping in Couples with a Child with Autism Spectrum Disorder," 3567–69.

11. Bobo H. Lau and Cecilia Cheng, "Gratitude and Coping among Familial Caregivers of Persons with Dementia," *Aging and Mental Health* 21, no. 4 (2017): 445–53, https://doi.org/10.1080/13607863.2015.1114588.

12. Alan E. Fruzzetti and Kate M. Iverson, "Mindfulness, Acceptance, Validation, and Individual Psychopathology in Couples," in *Mindfulness and Acceptance: Expanding the Cognitive-Behavioral Tradition*, edited by Steven C. Hayes, Victoria M. Follette, and Marsha M. Linehan (New York: Guilford Press, 2004), 172.

13. Hossein Keshavarz-Afshar et al., "Relationships between Attachment to God and Marital Satisfaction, and Mental Health in Parents of Children with Special Needs," *International Journal of Behavioral Sciences* 10, no. 1 (2016): 35–39; Gene G. Ano and Erin B. Vasconcelles, "Religious Coping and Psychological Adjustment in Stress: A Meta-Analysis," *Journal of Clinical Psychology* 61, no. 4 (October 2005): 461–80, https://doi.org/10.1002/jclp.20049.

14. Johnson and Piercy, "Exploring Partner Intimacy among Couples Raising Children on the Autism Spectrum," 646; Jeffrey P. Dew, Jeremy E. Uecker, and Brian J. Willoughby, "Joint Religiosity and Married Couples' Sexual Satisfaction," *Psychology of Religion and Spirituality* 12, no. 2 (2020): 201–12, https://doi.org/10.1037/rel0000243; Sheila Wray Gregoire, Rebecca Gregoire Lindenbach, and Joanna Sawatsky, *The Great Sex Rescue: The Lies You've Been Taught and How to Recover What God Intended* (Grand Rapids: Baker, 2021), 10.

15. Keshavarz-Afshar et al., "Relationships between Attachment to God and Marital Satisfaction, and Mental Health in Parents of Children with Special Needs," 35.

16. Anna M. Bujnowska et al., "Parenting and Future Anxiety: The Impact of Having a Child with Developmental Disabilities," *International Journal of Environmental Research and Public Health* 16, no. 4 (March 2019): 1–16, https://doi.org/10.3390/ijerph16040668; Vered Shenaar-Golan, "Hope and Subjective

Well-Being among Parents of Children with Special Needs," *Child and Family Social Work* 22, no. 1 (February 2017): 306–16, https://doi.org/10.1111/cfs.12241; Angela Sim et al., "Viewpoints on What Is Important to Maintain Relationship Satisfaction in Couples Raising a Child with Autism Spectrum Disorder," *Research in Autism Spectrum Disorders* 65 (September 2019): 1–13, https://doi.org /10.1016/j.rasd.2019.04.008.

17. Jon Kabat-Zinn, "Mindfulness," *Mindfulness* 6 (December 2015): 1481–83, https://doi.org/10.1007/s12671-015-0456-x.

18. Kirk W. Brown and Richard M. Ryan, "The Benefits of Being Present: Mindfulness and Its Role in Psychological Well-Being," *Journal of Personality and Social Psychology* 84, no. 4 (April 2003): 822–48, https://doi.org/10.1037/0022 -3514.84.4.822.

19. Rita Benn et al., "Mindfulness Training Effects for Parents and Educators of Children with Special Needs," *Developmental Psychology* 48, no. 5 (September 2012): 1476–87, https://doi.org/10.1037/a0027537; Brown and Ryan, "Benefits of Being Present," 822.

20. Nirbhay N. Singh et al., "Using Mindfulness to Improve Quality of Life in Caregivers of Individuals with Intellectual Disabilities and Autism Spectrum Disorder," *International Journal of Developmental Disabilities* 66, no. 5 (2020): 370–80, https://doi.org/10.1080/20473869.2020.1827211; Bazzano et al., "Mindfulness Based Stress Reduction (MBSR) for Parents and Caregivers of Individuals with Developmental Disabilities," 306; Benn et al., "Mindfulness Training Effects for Parents and Educators of Children with Special Needs,"1482–84; Manika Petcharat and Patricia Liehr, "Mindfulness Training for Parents of Children with Special Needs: Guidance for Nurses in Mental Health Practice," *Journal of Child and Adolescent Psychiatric Nursing* 30, no. 1 (February 2017): 35–46, https://doi .org/10.1111/jcap.12169.

21. Laura Eubanks Gambrel and Fred P. Piercy, "Mindfulness-Based Relationship Education for Couples Expecting Their First Child—Part 2: Phenomenological Findings," *Journal of Marital and Family Therapy* 41, no. 1 (January 2015): 25–41, https://doi.org/10.1111/jmft.12065; Jon Kabat-Zinn and Myla Kabat-Zinn, "Mindful Parenting: Perspectives on the Heart of the Matter," *Mindfulness* 12 (January 2021): 266–68, https://doi.org/10.1007/s12671-020-01564-7; Justin Parent and Karissa DiMarzio, "Advancing Mindful Parenting Research: An Introduction," *Mindfulness* 12 (January 2021): 261–65, https://doi.org/10.1007/s12671 -020-01572-7.

22. Fernando Garzon and Kristy Ford, "Adapting Mindfulness for Conservative Christians," *Journal of Psychology and Christianity* 35, no. 3 (2016): 263–68; Fernando Garzon et al., "Christian Accommodative Mindfulness: Definition, Current Research, and Group Protocol," *Religions* 13, no. 1 (2022): 63, https:// doi.org/10.3390/rel13010063; Veronica L. Timbers and Jennifer C. Hollenberger, "Christian Mindfulness and Mental Health: Coping through Sacred Traditions and Embodied Awareness," *Religions* 13, no. 1 (2022): 1–13, https://doi.org/10 .3390/rel13010062.

23. Kristy Ford and Fernando Garzon, "Research Note: A Randomized Investigation of Evangelical Christian Accommodative Mindfulness," *Spirituality in Clinical Practice* 4, no. 2 (2017): 92–99, https://doi.org/10.1037/scp0000137.

24. Scott H. Symington and Melissa F. Symington, "A Christian Model of Mindfulness: Using Mindfulness Principles to Support Psychological Well-Being, Value-Based Behavior, and the Christian Spiritual Journey," *Journal of Psychology and Christianity* 31, no. 1 (2012): 71–77.

25. Brother Lawrence, *The Practice of the Presence of God*, edited by Hal M. Helms, translated by Robert J. Edmonson (Brewster, MA: Paraclete Press, 1985), 146.

26. Friederike Winter et al., "Mindfulness-Based Couple Interventions: A Systematic Literature Review," *Family Process* 60, no. 3 (September 2021): 694–711, https://doi.org/10.1111/famp.12683; Benn et. al., "Mindfulness Training Effects for Parents and Educators of Children with Special Needs," 1484; Sean Barnes et al., "The Role of Mindfulness in Romantic Relationship Satisfaction and Responses to Relationship Stress," *Journal of Marital and Family Therapy* 33, no. 4 (October 2007): 482–500, https://doi.org/10.1111/j.1752-0606.2007.00033.x; Gambrel and Piercy, "Mindfulness-Based Relationship Education for Couples Expecting Their First Child," 33–34.

27. Nikko S. Da Paz and Jan L. Wallander, "Interventions That Target Improvements in Mental Health for Parents of Children with Autism Spectrum Disorders: A Narrative Review," *Clinical Psychology Review* 51 (February 2017): 1–14, https://doi.org/10.1016/j.cpr.2016.10.006; Bazzano et al., "Mindfulness Based Stress Reduction (MBSR) for Parents and Caregivers of Individuals with Developmental Disabilities," 299.

28. Jamie C. Brehaut et al., "Changes over Time in the Health of Caregivers of Children with Health Problems: Growth-Curve Findings from a 10-Year Canadian Population-Based Study," *American Journal of Public Health* 101, no. 12 (December 2011): 2308–316, https://doi.org/10.2105/AJPH.2011.300298; Brehaut et al., "Using Canadian Administrative Health Data to Examine the Health of Caregivers of Children with and without Health Problems," 1–2; Amy M. Smith and Joseph G. Grzywacz, "Health and Well-Being in Midlife Parents of Children with Special Health Needs," *Family, Systems, & Health* 32, no. 3 (September 2014), 303–12, https://doi.org/10.1037/fsh0000049.

29. Johnson and Piercy, "Exploring Partner Intimacy among Couples Raising Children on the Autism Spectrum," 654.

30. Sim et al., "Viewpoints on What Is Important to Maintain Relationship Satisfaction in Couples Raising a Child with Autism Spectrum Disorder," 3–4.

31. Janet Robertson et al., "The Impacts of Short Break Provision on Families with a Disabled Child: An International Literature Review," *Health and Social Care in the Community* 19, no. 4 (July 2011): 337–71, https://doi.org/10.1111/j.1365-2524.2010.00977.x; Peer and Hillman, "Stress and Resilience for Parents of Children with Intellectual and Developmental Disabilities," 96.

32. Felipe Barreto Schuch and Brendon Stubbs, "The Role of Exercise in Preventing and Treating Depression," *Current Sports Medicine Reports* 18, no. 8 (August 2019): 299–304, https://doi.org/10.1249/JSR.0000000000000620; Sheila Menon and Vidya Bhagat, "Literature Study on the Efficacy of Antidepressants with CBT in the Treatment of Depression," *Research Journal of Pharmacy and Technology* 15, no. 6 (June 2022): 275–87, https://doi.org/10.52711/0974-360x.2022.00465.

33. Katie E. Cherry et al., "Spirituality, Humor, and Resilience after Natural and Technological Disasters," *Journal of Nursing Scholarship* 50, no. 5 (July 2018): 492–501, https://doi.org/10.1111/jnu.12400; Mendez et al., "Fostering Resilience among Couples Coparenting a Young Child with Autism," 171; Alicja Rieger and J. Patrick McGrail, "Coping Humor and Family Functioning in Parents of Children with Disabilities," *Rehabilitation Psychology* 58, no. 1 (2013): 89–97, https://doi.org/10.1037/a0031556.

34. Mayo Clinic Staff, "Healthy Lifestyle Stress Management: Stress Relief from Laughter? It's No Joke," Mayo Clinic, accessed March 30, 2023, https://www.mayoclinic.org/healthy-lifestyle/stress-management/in-depth/stress-relief/art-20044456; Laura E. Marshak and Fran Pollock Prezant, *Married with Special-Needs Children* (Bethesda, MD: Woodbine House, 2007), 152.

Chapter 5 Check In with One Another

1. Sigan L. Hartley, Leann S. DaWalt, and Haley M. Schultz, "Daily Couple Experiences and Parent Affect in Families of Children with Versus without Autism," *Journal of Autism and Developmental Disorders* 47, no. 6 (June 2017): 1645–58, https://doi.org/10.1007/s10803-017-3088-2.

2. John M. Gottman et al., "Predicting Marital Happiness and Stability from Newlywed Interactions," *Journal of Marriage and the Family* 60, no. 1 (February 1998): 5–22; Hartley, DaWalt, and Schultz, "Daily Couple Experiences and Parent Affect in Families of Children with Versus without Autism," 1646.

3. Hartley, DaWalt, and Schultz, "Daily Couple Experiences and Parent Affect in Families of Children with Versus without Autism," 1655.

4. Gottman and Silver, *Seven Principles for Making Marriage Work*, 22.

5. Ramisch, Onaga, and Min Oh, "Keeping a Sound Marriage," 981.

6. Mendez et al., "Fostering Resilience among Couples Coparenting a Young Child with Autism," 171.

7. Fruzzetti and Iverson, "Mindfulness, Acceptance, Validation, and Individual Psychopathology in Couples," 171, 173, 183.

8. Hartley, DaWalt, and Schultz, "Daily Couple Experiences and Parent Affect in Families of Children with Versus Without Autism," 1655.

9. Fruzzetti and Iverson, "Mindfulness, Acceptance, Validation, and Individual Psychopathology in Couples," 171.

10. Les Parrott and Leslie Parrott, *Love Talk: Speak Each Other's Language Like You Never Have Before* (Grand Rapids: Zondervan, 2004).

11. Parrott and Parrott, *Love Talk*, 105–7.

12. Ramisch, Onaga, and Min Oh, "Keeping a Sound Marriage," 982; Pelchat, Lefebvre, and Levert, "Gender Differences and Similarities in the Experience of Parenting a Child with a Health Problem," 120; Christelle Vernhet et al., "Coping Strategies of Parents of Children with Autism Spectrum Disorder: A Systematic Review," *European Child & Adolescent Psychiatry* 28 (June 2019): 747–58, https://doi.org/10.1007/s00787-018-1183-3.

13. Fruzzetti and Iverson, "Mindfulness, Acceptance, Validation, and Individual Psychopathology in Couples," 171–72; Johnson and Piercy, "Exploring Partner Intimacy among Couples Raising Children on the Autism Spectrum," 654.

14. Fruzzetti and Iverson, "Mindfulness, Acceptance, Validation, and Individual Psychopathology in Couples," 173.

15. Johnson and Piercy, "Exploring Partner Intimacy among Couples Raising Children on the Autism Spectrum," 653; Duncan, Coatsworth, and Greenberg, "Model of Mindful Parenting," 258.

16. Hartley et al., "Couple Conflict in Parents of Children with versus without Autism: Self-Reported and Observed Findings," 2153.

17. Johnson and Piercy, "Exploring Partner Intimacy among Couples Raising Children on the Autism Spectrum," 653; Park and Lee, "Moderating Effect of Social Support on Parental Stress and Depression in Mothers of Children with Disabilities," 1; Gottman and Silver, *Seven Principles for Making Marriage Work*, 140.

18. Dew, Uecker, and Willoughby, "Joint Religiosity and Married Couples' Sexual Satisfaction," 204.

19. Hartley et al., "Couple Conflict in Parents of Children with versus without Autism: Self-Reported and Observed Findings," 2151.

20. Gottman and Silver, *Seven Principles for Making Marriage Work*, 138.

21. John Gottman and Joan DeClaire, *The Relationship Cure: A 5 Step Guide to Strengthening Your Marriage, Family, and Friendships* (New York: Three Rivers Press, 2001), 15.

22. Fruzzetti and Iverson, "Mindfulness, Acceptance, Validation, and Individual Psychopathology in Couples," 171, 187; Gottman and Silver, *Seven Principles for Making Marriage Work*, 158–59.

23. Thomas Gordon, *Parent Effectiveness Training: The Tested New Way to Raise Responsible Children* (New York: Peter H. Wyden, 1970).

24. Barnes et al., "Role of Mindfulness in Romantic Relationship Satisfaction and Responses to Relationship Stress," 495.

Chapter 6 Tackle Problems Together

1. Havva Gül and Çağla Gür, "The Relationship among Problem-Solving, Coping Styles and Stress Levels of Parents of Children with Autism Spectrum Disorder, Attention Deficit Hyperactivity Disorder and Typical Development," *European Journal of Educational Research* 11, no. 3 (July 2022): 1231–43, https://doi.org/10.12973/eu-jer.11.3.1231.

2. Fruzzetti and Iverson, "Mindfulness, Acceptance, Validation, and Individual Psychopathology in Couples," 180; Gül and Gür, "Relationship among Problem-Solving, Coping Styles and Stress Levels of Parents of Children with Autism Spectrum Disorder, Attention Deficit Hyperactivity Disorder and Typical Development," 1232.

3. Peer and Hillman, "Stress and Resilience for Parents of Children with Intellectual and Developmental Disabilities," 94; Lau and Cheng, "Gratitude and Coping among Familial Caregivers of Persons with Dementia," 446; M. Pilar Matud, "Gender Differences in Stress and Coping Styles," *Personality and Individual Differences* 37, no. 7 (November 2004): 1401–15, https://doi.org/10.1016/j.paid.2004.01.010; McConnell and Savage, "Stress and Resilience among Families Caring for Children with Intellectual Disability," 105.

4. Ana Miranda et al., "Parenting Stress in Mothers of Children with Autism without Intellectual Disability: Mediation of Behavioral Problems and Coping Strategies," *Frontiers in Psychology* 10 (March 2019): 1–12, https://doi.org/10.3389/fpsyg.2019.00464; Peer and Hillman, "Stress and Resilience for Parents of Children with Intellectual and Developmental Disabilities," 94.

5. Sim et al., "Relationship Satisfaction and Dyadic Coping in Couples with a Child with Autism Spectrum Disorder," 3566, 3569; Negash et al., "Intimacy in the Midst of Caregiving," 192.

6. McConnell and Savage, "Stress and Resilience among Families Caring for Children with Intellectual Disability," 105; Éadaoin Slattery, Jennifer McMahon, and Stephen Gallagher, "Optimism and Benefit Finding in Parents of Children with Developmental Disabilities: The Role of Positive Reappraisal and Social Support," *Research in Developmental Disabilities* 65 (June 2017): 12–22, https://doi.org/10.1016/j.ridd.2017.04.006; Peer and Hillman, "Stress and Resilience for Parents of Children with Intellectual and Developmental Disabilities," 94.

Chapter 7 Find Shelter in One Another

1. Mary B. Coughlin and Kristen A. Sethares, "Chronic Sorrow in Parents of Children with a Chronic Illness or Disability: An Integrative Literature Review," *Journal of Pediatric Nursing* 37 (November 2017): 108–16, https://doi.org/10.1016/j.pedn.2017.06.011.

2. C. Lindström, J. Aman, and Al Norberg, "Increased Prevalence of Burnout Symptoms in Parents of Chronically Ill Children," *Acta Paediatrica* 99, no. 3 (March 2010): 427–32, https://doi.org/10.1111/j.1651-2227.2009.01586.x; Jorge Bravo-Benítez et al., "Grief Experiences in Family Caregivers of Children with Autism Spectrum Disorder (ASD)," *International Journal of Environmental Research and Public Health* 16, no. 23 (November 2019): 4821, https://doi.org/10.3390/ijerph16234821.

3. Kaitlin Jeter and Brie Turns, "Grieving the Child That Never Was: Treatment of Ambiguous Loss in Parents of Children with Down Syndrome," *Australian and New Zealand Journal of Family Therapy* 43, no. 2 (June 2022): 243–56, https://doi.org/10.1002/anzf.1488.

4. Elisabeth Kübler-Ross, *On Death and Dying* (New York: Macmillan, 1969).

5. Bravo-Benítez et al., "Grief Experiences in Family Caregivers of Children with Autism Spectrum Disorder (ASD)," 4821.

6. Simon Olshansky, "Chronic Sorrow: A Response to Having a Mentally Defective Child," *Families in Society: The Journal of Contemporary Social Services* 43, no. 4 (April 1962): 190–93; Coughlin and Sethares, "Chronic Sorrow in Parents of Children with a Chronic Illness or Disability," 108; Bravo-Benítez et al., "Grief Experiences in Family Caregivers of Children with Autism Spectrum Disorder (ASD)," 2.

7. Bogdanna Andreyko, "The Emotional State of Parents in the Structure of the Stages of the Experience of Having a Child with Developmental Disabilities," *Journal of Education Culture and Society* 7, no. 2 (2016): 150–57, https://doi.org/10.15503/jecs20162.150.157; Raman Krishnan, Paul S. Russell, and Sushila Russell, "A Focus Group Study to Explore Grief Experiences among Parents of

Children with Autism Spectrum Disorder," *Journal of the Indian Academy of Applied Psychology* 43, no. 2 (July 2017): 267–75; Bravo-Benítez et al., "Grief Experiences in Family Caregivers of Children with Autism Spectrum Disorder (ASD)," 2.

8. Batchelor and Duke, "Chronic Sorrow in Parents with Chronically Ill Children,"164.

9. Ken Moses, "The Impact of Childhood Disability: The Parent's Struggle," *WAYS Magazine* 1 (1987): 6–10.

10. Tali Heiman, "Parents' Voice: Parents' Emotional and Practical Coping with a Child with Special Needs," *Psychology* 12, no. 5 (May 2021): 675–91, https://doi .org/10.4236/psych.2021.125042.

11. Marie Brien-Bérard and Catherine des Rivières-Pigeon, "Coping Strategies and the Marital Relationship among Parents Raising Children with ASD," *Journal of Child and Family Studies* 32 (March 2023): 908–25, https://doi.org /10.1007/s10826-022-02332-y; Jacqueline Corcoran, Amber Berry, and Stephanie Hill, "The Lived Experience of US Parents of Children with Autism Spectrum Disorders: A Systematic Review and Meta-Synthesis," *Journal of Intellectual Disabilities* 19, no. 4 (2015): 356–66, https://doi.org/10.1177/174462951557 7876.

12. Da Paz et al., "Acceptance or Despair?," 1979.

13. Liora Findler, Ayelet K. Jacoby, and Lidia Gabis, "Subjective Happiness among Mothers of Children with Disabilities: The Role of Stress, Attachment, Guilt and Social Support," *Research in Developmental Disabilities* no. 55 (August 2016): 44–54, https://doi.org/10.1016/j.ridd.2016.03.006; Da Paz et al., "Acceptance or Despair?," 1979.

14. Coughlin and Sethares, "Chronic Sorrow in Parents of Children with a Chronic Illness or Disability," 109.

15. Coughlin and Sethares, "Chronic Sorrow in Parents of Children with a Chronic Illness or Disability," 109–12.

16. Coughlin and Sethares, "Chronic Sorrow in Parents of Children with a Chronic Illness or Disability," 114.

17. Leah Jones et al., "Gender Differences When Parenting Children with Autism Spectrum Disorders: A Multilevel Modeling Approach," *Journal of Autism and Developmental Disorders* 43 (September 2013): 2090–98, https://doi.org/10 .1007/s10803-012-1756-9.

18. Ujianti, "Role of Support Group for Parents of Children with Special Needs," 32.

19. Matud, "Gender Differences in Stress and Coping Styles," 1411; Pelchat, Lefebvre, and Levert, "Gender Differences and Similarities in the Experience of Parenting a Child with a Health Problem," 120.

20. Barnett et al., "Building New Dreams," 194.

21. Ujianti, "Role of Support Group for Parents of Children with Special Needs," 36.

22. Kimberly L. Gajeton, "Religious Coping and Spiritual Struggles in Parents of Children with Autism Spectrum Disorder," PhD diss., Regent University, 2015, ProQuest (3700826), iii.

Chapter 8 Stop to Rest Together

1. Lindström, Aman, and Norberg, "Increased Prevalence of Burnout Symptoms in Parents of Chronically Ill Children," 427, 430.

2. Lindström, Aman, and Norberg, "Increased Prevalence of Burnout Symptoms in Parents of Chronically Ill Children," 427, 430–31.

3. Marshak and Prezant, *Married with Special-Needs Children*, 97; Johnson and Piercy, "Exploring Partner Intimacy among Couples Raising Children on the Autism Spectrum," 653.

4. Brien-Bérard and des Rivières-Pigeon, "Coping Strategies and the Marital Relationship among Parents Raising Children with ASD," 909.

5. Peer and Hillman, "Stress and Resilience for Parents of Children with Intellectual and Developmental Disabilities," 96; Robertson et al., "Impacts of Short Break Provision on Families with a Disabled Child," 363–64.

6. Fruzzetti and Iverson, "Mindfulness, Acceptance, Validation, and Individual Psychopathology in Couples," 181–82.

Chapter 9 Enjoy One Another on the Journey

1. Johnson and Piercy, "Exploring Partner Intimacy among Couples Raising Children on the Autism Spectrum," 646.

2. Hartley, DaWalt, and Schultz, "Daily Couple Experiences and Parent Affect in Families of Children with Versus without Autism," 1656.

3. Gregoire, Lindenbach, and Sawatsky, *Great Sex Rescue*, 13; Clifford Penner and Joyce Penner, *The Gift of Sex: A Guide to Sexual Fulfillment* (Nashville: W Publishing Group, 2003), 28–29.

4. Gottman and Silver, *Seven Principles for Making Marriage Work*, 223.

5. Marshak and Prezant, *Married with Special-Needs Children*, 99.

6. Gregoire, Lindenbach, and Sawatsky, *Great Sex Rescue*, 216.

7. Johnson and Piercy, "Exploring Partner Intimacy among Couples Raising Children on the Autism Spectrum," 644, 649.

8. Negash et al., "Intimacy in the Midst of Caregiving," 195.

9. Negash et al., "Intimacy in the Midst of Caregiving," 194–95; Marshak and Prezant, *Married with Special-Needs Children*, 97–98.

10. Penner and Penner, *Gift of Sex*, 95; Negash et al., "Intimacy in the Midst of Caregiving," 194; Emily Nagoski, *Come As You Are: The Surprising New Science That Will Transform Your Sex Life* (New York: Simon & Schuster, 2015), 117; Sigan L. Hartley, Lauren M. Papp, and Daniel Bolt, "Spillover of Marital Interactions and Parenting Stress in Families of Children with Autism Spectrum Disorder," *Journal of Clinical Child & Adolescent Psychology* 47, no. S1 (November 2018): S88–99, https://doi.org/10.1080/15374416.2016.1152552.

11. Lisa D. Hamilton and Cindy M. Meston, "Chronic Stress and Sexual Function in Women," *Journal of Sexual Medicine* 10, no. 10 (2013): 2443–54, https://doi.org/10.1111/jsm.12249.

12. Marshak and Prezant, *Married with Special-Needs Children*, 105.

13. Nagoski, *Come As You Are*, 149.

14. Nagoski, *Come As You Are*, 121.

15. Marshak and Prezant, *Married with Special-Needs Children,* 98; Brien-Bérard and des Rivières-Pigeon, "Coping Strategies and the Marital Relationship among Parents Raising Children with ASD," 915.

16. Nagoski, *Come As You Are,* 122.

17. Nagoski, *Come As You Are,* 133.

18. Negash et al., "Intimacy in the Midst of Caregiving," 194.

19. Gregoire, Lindenbach, and Sawatsky, *Great Sex Rescue,* 102, 107–8.

20. Gottman and Silver, *Seven Principles for Making Marriage Work,* 199.

21. Gregoire, Lindenbach, and Sawatsky, *Great Sex Rescue,* 103–5.

22. Marshak and Prezant, *Married with Special-Needs Children,* 105.

23. Gregoire, Lindenbach, and Sawatsky, *Great Sex Rescue,* 123.

24. Parrott and Parrott, *Love Talk,* 109.

25. Penner and Penner, *Gift of Sex,* 248.

26. Nagoski, *Come As You Are,* 122; Penner and Penner, *Gift of Sex,* 95; Marshak and Prezant, *Married with Special-Needs Children,* 106.

27. Penner and Penner, *Gift of Sex,* 22.

Chapter 10 Find Others to Travel Beside

1. Corcoran, Berry, and Hill, "Lived Experience of US Parents of Children with Autism Spectrum Disorders," 362; Wattana Tejakum et al., "Depressive Symptoms, Social Support, Cognitive Function, and Stigma: Predictors of Resilience in Caregivers of Children with Intellectual Disabilities," *Frontiers of Nursing* 9, no. 4 (December 2022): 361–69, https://doi.org/10.2478/fon-2022-0046.

2. Peer and Hillman, "Stress and Resilience for Parents of Children with Intellectual and Developmental Disabilities," 95; Johnson and Piercy, "Exploring Partner Intimacy among Couples Raising Children on the Autism Spectrum," 654.

3. Park and Lee, "Moderating Effect of Social Support on Parental Stress and Depression in Mothers of Children with Disabilities," 2; Slattery, McMahon, and Gallagher, "Optimism and Benefit Finding in Parents of Children with Developmental Disabilities," 14.

4. Peer and Hillman, "Stress and Resilience for Parents of Children with Intellectual and Developmental Disabilities," 95–96; Johnson and Piercy, "Exploring Partner Intimacy among Couples Raising Children on the Autism Spectrum," 654.

5. Zainab Suntai, Kirsten Laha-Walsh, and David L. Albright, "Effectiveness of Remote Interventions in Improving Caregiver Stress Outcomes for Caregivers of People with Traumatic Brain Injury," *Rehabilitation Psychology* 66, no. 4 (2021): 415–22, https://doi.org/10.1037/rep0000402.

6. Ujianti, "Role of Support Group for Parents of Children with Special Needs," 36.

7. Barnett et al., "Building New Dreams," 195.

8. Ujianti, "Role of Support Group for Parents of Children with Special Needs," 33–34; Pelchat, Lefebvre, and Levert, "Gender Differences and Similarities in the Experience of Parenting a Child with a Health Problem," 120–21.

9. Institute for Family Studies, "The Ties That Bind: Is Faith a Global Force for Good or Ill in the Family?" Institute for Family Studies, accessed August 14, 2023, https://ifstudies.org/reports/world-family-map/2019/executive-summary;

Tyler J. VanderWeele, "Religious Service Attendance, Marriage, and Health," *Institute for Family Studies* (blog), November 29, 2016, https://ifstudies.org/blog/religious-service-attendance-marriage-and-health.

Chapter 11 Have One Another's Backs

1. Amy S. Weitlauf et al., "Relationship Satisfaction, Parenting Stress, and Depression in Mothers of Children with Autism," *Autism* 18, no. 2 (February 2014): 194–98, https://doi.org/10.1177/1362361312458039; Ramisch, Onaga, and Min Oh, "Keeping a Sound Marriage," 975.

2. Michelle Beer, Lynn Ward, and Kathryn Moar, "The Relationship between Mindful Parenting and Distress in Parents of Children with an Autism Spectrum Disorder," *Mindfulness* 4 (January 2013): 102–12, https://doi.org/10.1007/s12671-012-0192-4; Nathaniel Scherer, Ibone Verhey, and Hannah Kuper, "Depression and Anxiety in Parents of Children with Intellectual and Developmental Disabilities: A Systematic Review and Meta-Analysis," *PLoS One* 14, no. 7 (July 2019), https://doi.org/10.1371/journal.pone.0219888; McConnell and Savage, "Stress and Resilience among Families Caring for Children with Intellectual Disability," 101.

3. Hartley, Papp, and Bolt, "Spillover of Marital Interactions and Parenting Stress in Families of Children with Autism Spectrum Disorder," S95; Weitlauf et al., "Relationship Satisfaction, Parenting Stress, and Depression in Mothers of Children with Autism," 195.

4. Mendez et al., "Fostering Resilience among Couples Coparenting a Young Child with Autism," 172–73.

5. MacDonald and Hastings, "Mindful Parenting and Care Involvement of Fathers of Children with Intellectual Disabilities," 236.

6. Coughlin and Sethares, "Chronic Sorrow in Parents of Children with a Chronic Illness or Disability," 114.

7. Scherer, Verhey, and Kuper, "Depression and Anxiety in Parents of Children with Intellectual and Developmental Disabilities," 3; MacDonald and Hastings, "Mindful Parenting and Care Involvement of Fathers of Children with Intellectual Disabilities," 236.

8. Hartley, Papp, and Bolt, "Spillover of Marital Interactions and Parenting Stress in Families of Children with Autism Spectrum Disorder," S95; Park and Lee, "Moderating Effect of Social Support on Parental Stress and Depression in Mothers of Children with Disabilities," 2; Lindström, Aman, and Norberg, "Increased Prevalence of Burnout Symptoms in Parents of Chronically Ill Children," 431.

9. Jones et al., "Gender Differences When Parenting Children with Autism Spectrum Disorders," 2090, 2095; Findler, Jacoby, and Gabis, "Subjective Happiness among Mothers of Children with Disabilities," 46; Brien-Bérard and des Rivières-Pigeon, "Coping Strategies and the Marital Relationship among Parents Raising Children with ASD," 917.

10. Hartley, Papp, and Bolt, "Spillover of Marital Interactions and Parenting Stress in Families of Children with Autism Spectrum Disorder," S96.

11. Johnson and Piercy, "Exploring Partner Intimacy among Couples Raising Children on the Autism Spectrum," 651.

12. Sim et al., "Relationship Satisfaction and Dyadic Coping in Couples with a Child with Autism Spectrum Disorder," 3569.

13. Mendez et al., "Fostering Resilience among Couples Coparenting a Young Child with Autism," 166.

14. McConnell and Savage, "Stress and Resilience among Families Caring for Children with Intellectual Disability," 106.

15. Nigela Ahemaitijiang et al., "A Review of Mindful Parenting: Theory, Measurement, Correlates, and Outcomes," *Journal of Pacific Rim Psychology*, 15 (August 2021): 1–20, https://doi.org/10.1177/18344909211037016.

16. Ahemaitijiang et al., "Review of Mindful Parenting," 2.

17. Petcharat and Liehr, "Mindfulness Training for Parents of Children with Special Needs," 35; Koa Whittingham, "Parents of Children with Disabilities, Mindfulness and Acceptance: A Review and Call for Research," *Mindfulness* 5 (December 2014): 704–9, https://doi.org/10.1007/s12671-013-0224-8; Duncan, Coatsworth, and Greenberg, "Model of Mindful Parenting," 263.

18. Mahdiyeh Behbahani et al., "Effects of Mindful Parenting Training on Clinical Symptoms in Children with Attention Deficit Hyperactivity Disorder and Parenting Stress: Randomized Controlled Trial," *Iranian Journal of Medical Sciences* 43, no. 6 (November 2018): 596–604; Ahemaitijiang et al., "Review of Mindful Parenting," 13; Beer, Ward, and Moar, "Relationship between Mindful Parenting and Distress in Parents of Children with an Autism Spectrum Disorder," 103.

19. Duncan, Coatsworth, and Greenberg, "Model of Mindful Parenting," 261, 263; Bazzano et al., "Mindfulness Based Stress Reduction (MBSR) for Parents and Caregivers of Individuals with Developmental Disabilities," 299.

20. Kabat-Zinn and Kabat-Zinn, "Mindful Parenting," 268; Duncan, Coatsworth, and Greenberg, "Model of Mindful Parenting," 258–60; Ahemaitijiang et al., "Review of Mindful Parenting," 2–3; Beer, Ward, and Moar, "Relationship between Mindful Parenting and Distress in Parents of Children with an Autism Spectrum Disorder," 103.

21. Kabat-Zinn and Kabat-Zinn, "Mindful Parenting," 266.

22. Jessica L. Fuller and Elizabeth A. Fitter, "Mindful Parenting: A Behavioral Tool for Parent Well-Being," *Behavior Analysis in Practice* 13, no. 4 (2020): 767–71, https://doi.org/10.1007/s40617-020-00447-6.

23. We have here combined and modified two exercises: Phang Cheng Kar, Keng Shian-Ling, and Chiang Khai Chong, "Mindful-S.T.O.P.: Mindfulness Made Easy for Stress Reduction in Medical Students," *Education in Medicine Journal* 6, no. 2 (2014): 48–56, http://dx.doi.org/10.5959/eimj.v6i2.230; Marsha M. Linehan, "Distress Tolerance Handout 4: The STOP Skill," in *DBT Skills Training Handouts and Worksheets*, second edition (New York: Guilford Press, 2014), 327.

24. Ahemaitijiang et al., "Review of Mindful Parenting," 4.

25. Ryan Tobin and David M. Dunkley, "Self-Critical Perfectionism and Lower Mindfulness and Self-Compassion Predict Anxious and Depressive Symptoms over Two Years," *Behaviour Research and Therapy* 136 (January 2021): 1–12, https://doi.org/10.1016/j.brat.2020.103780.

26. D. W. Winnicott, *Babies and Their Mothers*, edited by Clare Winnicott, Ray Shepherd, and Madeleine Davis (Cambridge, MA: Perseus Publishing, 1987), 38.

27. Shwikar Othman et al., "Examining the Influence of Self-Compassion Education and Training upon Parents and Families When Caring for Their Children: A Systematic Review," *The Open Psychology Journal* 15, no. 1 (2022): 1–16, http://dx.doi.org/10.2174/18743501-v15-e221020-2022-39.

28. Duncan, Coatsworth, and Greenberg, "Model of Mindful Parenting," 260.

29. Bahareh Shahabi, Rana Shahabi, and Elham Foroozandeh, "Analysis of the Self-Compassion and Cognitive Flexibility with Marital Compatibility in Parents of Children with Autism Spectrum Disorder," *International Journal of Developmental Disabilities* 66, no. 4 (March 2020): 282–88, https://doi.org/10.1080/20473869.2019.1573000; Beer, Ward, and Moar, "Relationship between Mindful Parenting and Distress in Parents of Children with an Autism Spectrum Disorder," 110; Tobin and Dunkley, "Self-Critical Perfectionism and Lower Mindfulness and Self-Compassion Predict Anxious and Depressive Symptoms over Two Years," 9.

30. Kristin M. Sæther et al., "First-Time Parents' Experiences Related to Parental Self-Efficacy: A Scoping Review," *Research in Nursing & Health* 46, no. 1 (February 2023): 101–12, https://doi.org/10.1002/nur.22285.

Chapter 12 Call Out for Help

1. Scherer, Verhey, and Kuper, "Depression and Anxiety in Parents of Children with Intellectual and Developmental Disabilities," 12; Brehaut et al., "Using Canadian Administrative Health Data to Examine the Health of Caregivers of Children with and without Health Problems," 1; Smith and Grzywacz, "Health and Well-Being in Midlife Parents of Children with Special Health Needs," 305.

2. Scherer, Verhey, and Kuper, "Depression and Anxiety in Parents of Children with Intellectual and Developmental Disabilities," 12.

3. Scherer, Verhey, and Kuper, "Depression and Anxiety in Parents of Children with Intellectual and Developmental Disabilities," 12.

4. Bujnowska et al., "Parenting and Future Anxiety," 1.

5. McConnell and Savage, "Stress and Resilience among Families Caring for Children with Intellectual Disability," 100.

6. Maria A. Villarroel and Emily P. Terlizzi, "Symptoms of Depression among Adults: United States, 2019," *NCHS Data Brief* no. 379 (September 2020), https://www.cdc.gov/nchs/data/databriefs/db379-H.pdf.

7. Centers for Disease Control and Prevention (CDC), "Depression among Women," last reviewed May 22, 2023, CDC, https://www.cdc.gov/reproductivehealth/depression/index.htm#Postpartum.

8. Jones et al., "Gender Differences When Parenting Children with Autism Spectrum Disorders," 2095; Scherer, Verhey, and Kuper, "Depression and Anxiety in Parents of Children with Intellectual and Developmental Disabilities," 12; MacDonald and Hastings, "Mindful Parenting and Care Involvement of Fathers of Children with Intellectual Disabilities," 236; Park and Lee, "Moderating Effect of Social Support on Parental Stress and Depression in Mothers of Children with Disabilities," 2; Pelchat, Lefebvre, and Levert, "Gender Differences and Similarities in the Experience of Parenting a Child with a Health Problem," 118.

9. Rosa Vilaseca, Fina Ferrer, and Joan G. Olmos, "Gender Differences in Positive Perceptions, Anxiety, and Depression among Mothers and Fathers of

Children with Intellectual Disabilities: A Logistic Regression Analysis," *Quality & Quantity: International Journal of Methodology* 48 (July 2014): 2241–53, https://doi.org/10.1007/s11135-013-9889-2.

10. Martina Corsi et al., "PTSD in Parents of Children with Severe Diseases: A Systematic Review to Face COVID-19 Impact," *Italian Journal of Pediatrics* 47, no. 1 (January 2021): 1–7, https://doi.org/10.1186/s13052-021-00957-1; Martin Pinquart, "Posttraumatic Stress Symptoms and Disorders in Parents of Children and Adolescents with Chronic Physical Illnesses: A Meta-Analysis," *Journal of Traumatic Stress* 32, no. 1 (February 2019): 88–96, https://doi.org/10.1002/jts.22354.

11. Sim et al., "Relationship Satisfaction and Dyadic Coping in Couples with a Child with Autism Spectrum Disorder," 3568.

12. Park and Lee, "Moderating Effect of Social Support on Parental Stress and Depression in Mothers of Children with Disabilities," 2; Scherer, Verhey, and Kuper, "Depression and Anxiety in Parents of Children with Intellectual and Developmental Disabilities," 2.

13. National Institute of Mental Health, "Substance Use and Co-Occurring Mental Disorders," NIMH, accessed March 23, 2023, https://www.nimh.nih.gov/health/topics/substance-use-and-mental-health.

14. National Institute of Mental Health, "My Mental Health: Do I Need Help?," NIMH, accessed June 26, 2023, https://www.nimh.nih.gov/health/publications/my-mental-health-do-i-need-help; American Psychiatric Association, *Diagnostic and Statistical Manual of Mental Disorders (DSM-5-TR)*, fifth edition, text revision (Washington, DC: American Psychiatric Association Publishing, 2022), 183.

15. John L. Oliffe et al., "Men's Depression and Suicide," *Current Psychiatry Reports* 21, no. 10 (September 2019): 1–6, https://doi.org/10.1007/s11920-019-1088-y.

16. National Institute of Mental Health, "What Is Post-Traumatic Stress Disorder (PTSD)?" NIMH, May 2023, https://www.nimh.nih.gov/health/topics/post-traumatic-stress-disorder-ptsd.

17. Thirsa Conijn et al., "Reducing Posttraumatic Stress in Parents of Patients with a Rare Inherited Metabolic Disorder Using Eye Movement Desensitization and Reprocessing Therapy: A Case Study," *Orphanet Journal of Rare Diseases* 16 (March 2019): 1–6, https://doi.org/10.1186/s13023-021-01768-7; Deany Laliotis and Francine Shapiro, "EMDR Therapy for Trauma-Related Disorders," *Evidence Based Treatments for Trauma-Related Psychological Disorders: A Practical Guide for Clinicians*, second edition, edited by Ulrich Schnyder and Marylène Cloitre (New York: Springer, 2022), 227–54, https://doi.org/10.1007/978-3-030-97802-0_11; Elan Shapiro and Louise Maxfield, "The Efficacy of EMDR Early Interventions," *Journal of EMDR Practice and Research* 13, no. 4 (2019): 291–301, https://doi.org/10.1891/1933-3196.13.4.291.

18. Gottman and Silver, *Seven Principles for Making Marriage Work*, 10; Paul M. Spengler et al., "A Comprehensive Meta-Analysis on the Efficacy of Emotionally Focused Couple Therapy," *Couple and Family Psychology: Research and Practice* (September 2022): advanced online publication, https://doi.org/10.1037/cfp0000233; Kyle Benson, "Is It Time to Go for Couples Counseling?," *The*

Gottman Institute (blog), accessed March 23, 2023, https://www.gottman.com /blog/is-it-time-to-go-to-couples-counseling/.

19. Gottman and Silver, *Seven Principles for Making Marriage Work*, 10.

20. Michael J. McGuire and Adam C. Pace, "Self-Stigma of Depression in Christians versus the General Population," *Mental Health, Religion & Culture* 21, no. 6 (2018): 601–8, https://doi.org/10.1080/13674676.2018.1522623.

21. McGuire and Pace, "Self-Stigma of Depression in Christians versus the General Population," 604.

22. McGuire and Pace, "Self-Stigma of Depression in Christians versus the General Population," 604; Katharine S. Adams et al., "Relationship of Christian Beliefs to Attitudes toward People with Mental Illness," *American Journal of Psychotherapy* 71, no. 1 (November 2018): 104–9, https://doi.org/10.1176/appi .psychotherapy.20180022.

23. Sheila Menon and Vidya Bhagat, "Literature Study on the Efficacy of Antidepressants with CBT in the Treatment of Depression," 2776; Lynn Boschloo et al., "The Symptom-Specific Efficacy of Antidepressant Medication vs. Cognitive Behavioral Therapy in the Treatment of Depression: Results from an Individual Patient Data Meta-Analysis," *World Psychiatry* 18, no. 2 (June 2019): 183–91, https://doi.org/10.1002/wps.20630.

24. Gajeton, "Religious Coping and Spiritual Struggles in Parents of Children with Autism Spectrum Disorder," iii.

25. Joshua B. Grubbs et al., "Self, Struggle, and Soul: Linking Personality, Self-Concept, and Religious/Spiritual Struggle," *Personality and Individual Differences* 101 (October 2016): 144–52, https://doi.org/10.1016/j.paid.2016.05.365.

Chapter 13 Cultivate Joy along the Trail

1. Peer and Hillman, "Stress and Resilience for Parents of Children with Intellectual and Developmental Disabilities," 94–95; McConnell and Savage, "Stress and Resilience among Families Caring for Children with Intellectual Disability," 105.

2. Slattery, McMahon, and Gallagher, "Optimism and Benefit Finding in Parents of Children with Developmental Disabilities," 13; Frank D. Fincham and Ross W. May, "Generalized Gratitude and Prayers of Gratitude in Marriage," *The Journal of Positive Psychology* 16, no. 2 (2021): 282–87, https://doi.org/10.1080 /17439760.2020.1716053; Cameron L. Gordon, Robyn A. M. Arnette, and Rachel E. Smith, "Have You Thanked Your Spouse Today?: Felt and Expressed Gratitude among Married Couples," *Personality and Individual Differences* 50, no. 3 (2011): 339–43, https://psycnet.apa.org/doi/10.1016/j.paid.2010.10.012; Johnson and Piercy, "Exploring Partner Intimacy among Couples Raising Children on the Autism Spectrum," 654; Lau and Cheng, "Gratitude and Coping among Familial Caregivers of Persons with Dementia," 446; Jeffrey Kilbert et al., "The Impact of an Integrated Gratitude Intervention on Positive Affect and Coping Resources," *International Journal of Applied Positive Psychology* 3 (May 2019): 23–41, https:// doi.org/10.1007/s41042-019-00015-6.

About the Authors

TODD and **KRISTIN EVANS** are award-winning authors, speakers, and disability parents. They are passionate about empowering other parents of children with chronic illnesses and disabilities to thrive, as well as equipping ministry leaders and professionals to serve parent caregivers. They both earned their MA in Christian educational ministries at Wheaton College in Illinois and have served together in full-time ministry in church, camping, and retreat settings. Todd received his PhD from Vanderbilt University's School of Engineering and currently manages his own business. Kristin earned her MSW from the University of Tennessee and is a Licensed Master Social Worker experienced in couples, child and family, substance abuse, and crisis counseling. They enjoy traveling and the outdoors together.

Connect with Kristin and Todd:

DisabilityParenting.com

 @DisabilityParenting

 @Kristin.Evans.5895

@AuthorKristinEv